Songs and Prayers of the Church

Canticles and Intercessions for use
with the Daily Office and other occasions

Compiled by John Michael Mountney MA

Rector of the Parmentergate Team Ministry, Norwich,
and Warden of the Julian Shrine

MOWBRAY

Mowbray
A Cassell imprint
Villiers House, 41/47 Strand, London W C2N 5JE, England

Compilation © John Michael Mountney 1990
Please see Acknowledgements at the end of this book
for copyrights in certain material

First published 1990

ISBN 0-264-67189-9

Typeset in Compugraphic Palatino
Printed and bound in Great Britain by
Biddles Ltd, Guildford and King's Lynn

Foreword

In the period of liturgical revision from 1960 to 1980, the legacy of the Tractarian movement in England, combined with the insights of the liturgical movement on the Continent, focused attention almost exclusively on the Eucharist. Morning and Evening Prayer in the ASB have more the feel of Cranmer's Office in modern dress than a re-thought form.

But in the last decade or so, there has been a considerable interest in the Daily Office, or perhaps more accurately, in the more structured forms of non-eucharistic worship. For a start, there has been the growing awareness among lay people (as well as clergy) in all traditions of the need for a pattern of common daily prayer which would supplement and nourish the eucharistic worship of the Church on Sundays.

Second, while only a proportion of Christian people, and that includes the clergy, say a full Daily Office, most Christians pray, and a very large proportion include in their daily prayer an element of praise, the reading of Holy Scripture, and intercession. These are the elements that Christians of different traditions have in common, and we are beginning to realise that in our pattern of daily prayer we have more that unites than divides us.

What has emerged from common Christian conviction has been supported by recent liturgical scholarship. Over the last twenty years or so a stream of books and articles on the origins and development of the Daily Office has allowed us to see that the tremendous concentration on the recitation of the Psalter was a largely monastic tradition, while extended reading of Holy Scripture in course is a particular contribution of the Reformation. By contrast, the earliest tradition seems to have been focused on the praise of God and on intercessory prayer.

It is just these elements which have such popular appeal in, for example, the Daily Office at Taizé or – to take a rather different example – the services of Prayer and Praise in the more charismatic tradition.

As preparations for the revision of the ASB during the 1990s get under way, the Church of England has the opportunity for reconsidering and revising its pattern of morning and evening prayer, and contributions like Father Mountney's *Songs and Prayers of the Church* will be a valuable stimulus and enrichment during this period. While it is too early to say what direction the Church may take, there is an often-expressed need for a simple structure of daily prayer which clergy and lay people might have in common. A simple, basic structure surrounded by a rich forest of hymns and antiphons, canticles and responsories, intercessions and collects, would enable those who wished to say a full form of the Office to do so. But it would not make those who whether by temperament, tradition, or opportunity used no more than the basic skeleton feel that they were not playing their part equally in the common prayer of the people of God. For many people, an acclamation of praise, a biblical reading, a Gospel canticle and then a collect or conclusion to sum up a period of free prayer will be the appropriate diet.

For these reasons, Father Mountney's book is to be welcomed warmly. It has as its focus Prayer and Praise, expressed in the wide selection of biblical canticles, and a large number of patterns of intercession, so devised that they turn meditative reading and the praise of God into prayer. By the familiarity bred of repetition, canticles bed themselves in our minds; and the repeated use of certain canticles in certain seasons of the Church's year helps to provide a biblical bedrock to our less conscious praises. In the Office, we pattern ourselves and our prayer on scripture so that, as a Church, we absorb the tradition by rehearsing it. For too long we have made a rigid division between reciting the Psalter, listening to great tracts of Scripture and praying the intercessions after the Office is ended. It is clear that what will serve God's people best are forms which, while rooted and grounded in scripture, turn reading into reflection and reflection into prayer. With the help of *Songs and Prayers of the Church* this ideal comes more than a step closer.

David Stancliffe
Provost of Portsmouth
Ash Wednesday, 1990

Contents

For the Team

A✝M✝D✝G

Introduction

1 An Historical Perspective

Over the centuries the Divine Office has almost certainly been the Church of England's greatest liturgical strength, while the Communion was theologically unsatisfactory in many ways, and held a lower position in the worshipping life of the Church. Today we live in a reversed situation, for since the beginning of the Oxford Movement the Eucharist has steadily continued to work its way to the top of the liturgical programme to the point where it has both received maximum theological attention in *The Alternative Service Book* and has become the central act of worship for most parishes. By contrast the Divine Office has declined both as a priest's act of devotion and as the people's act of Sunday worship. It is significant that in the ASB the Daily Office appears to have received correspondingly less theological attention. This is not to decry in any way the advances in eucharistic worship that were clamouring to be made; rather the time has come for equal advances to be made for the Divine Office if it is to become once again, and in accordance with the Prayer Book's inspired hope, the basic daily prayer of the Church, that is, the prayer of her people. It is to this end that this book is humbly devoted, by the provision of extra canticles and intercessions.

The idea of using a scriptural canticle as well as the psalms in the Office is at least as old as the Benedictine Office of the sixth century. In the pre-Reformation Office an Old Testament canticle was provided as part of the psalmody for Lauds on every morning of the week. When the Book of Common Prayer was published and a new *cursus* of psalms provided, these canticles vanished with the exception of the *Benedicite* (the old Sunday canticle) but only as an alternative to the *Te Deum*. When the Roman Breviary was revised in the early 1970s the principle of this OT canticle, which it had never lost, was extended to provide a different one for each day of its four-week Psalter cycle. Moreover, in a novel way, New Testament canticles (from outside the Gospels) were also provided; these were to be used at Evening Prayer on each day of the week and repeated throughout the four-week Psalter. At no time were these canticles intended to be an *alternative* to the Gospel canticles, an arrangement advocated in the ASB echoing the BCP's provision of certain psalms as alternatives to the Gospel canticles.

Although the old canticles were lost to the BCP it is not without significance that in 1623 George Withers published his *Hymnes and Songs of the Church*, set to music by Orlando Gibbons. These were nothing more than versifications of the old Office canticles, and whilst the verses have vanished from use, the tunes are still to be found in our hymn books. The ASB has begun to make good this loss by providing a few alternative canticles alongside the Gospel canticles (*Benedictus, Magnificat, Nunc Dimittis*) at Morning and Evening Prayer in both standard and shorter forms. The inspiration for these was chiefly the Daily Office of the Joint Liturgical Group of 1967, which was revised and enlarged in 1978, so that the total number of canticles in liturgical use and available in 1980 greatly exceeded those provided in the ASB, and has increased since with the advent of such books as *Lent, Holy Week and Easter, Prayers and Services*. It has therefore been the aim of the present writer to gather between two covers as many of those canticles as possible, from a wide selection of contemporary liturgical sources, and arrange them for use at the appropriate seasons of the liturgical year. Care has been taken to provide canticles for mornings and evenings for each day of the week as well as at Seasons, and Greater and Lesser Holy Days in accordance with the ASB calendar. Inevitably, making full use of the material available has necessitated the dislocation of the scheme for weekdays in the ASB. An additional season, 'Before Advent', has been included from the seventh Sunday before Christmas, whilst among Lesser Holy Days, 'Of Any Saint' is expanded to include a section for Women saints. Another classification is given for Mystics. To Abbots are added Abbesses. A feast which has been growing in importance in many parishes in recent years, Christ the King (Fifth Sunday before Christmas), is also provided for in this book.

Historically speaking, the Divine Office has never been very strong on that other vital element of the totality of prayer, intercession; at least not in the Western Church, unless it be argued that intercession is the summation of the Office. In the Hour of Prime, now defunct, there were litanical prayers. In the BCP Cranmer provided the Litany, the *Kyrie eleison*, the suffrages and a large selection of collects to suit different occasions, to be used after the 'third collect'. The compilers of ASB broadly followed this pattern with little alteration. Here, surely is room for fresh thinking. The Taizé Office and the modern Roman Breviary have seized the opportunity presented by liturgical renewal and together offer a huge collection of short intercessions (many of which are reproduced in this book) to suit a wide variety of occasions. These intercessions also contain elements of thanksgiving and acclamation, without which the Office would be incomplete. The reader will also observe that they are in most cases heavily based on Scripture, the starting point of all prayer. If some phrases have a more than familiar ring, this is because all prayer should be rooted in a living tradition, and I regret not being able to draw more from the Orthodox East or the Celtic West. The shape and length of the intercessions to some extent resemble Cranmer's suffrages, but offer a repeating instead of a variable response for the people. But Cranmer's greatest contribution to intercession was perhaps in his provision of collects for particular occasions. Although the modern versions of these found in ASB may still, of course, be used, they remain essentially 'minister-centred'. The use of responsorial prayer, on the other hand, has the advantage of drawing the people more deeply into the prayer.

Finally, it must be stressed that the use of this book is not intended to be exclusive to the Office. It is very much hoped that it will be used as a resource for all who are in the habit of praying, and its treasures ought to be revealed to house groups and prayer groups, and used in family services and a host of occasions requiring the building blocks of worship. Users of this book ought not to overlook Holy Communion, Rite A, Note 20 and sections 1, 16 and 47, or Rite B, Note 12 and sections 11, 40 and 48. Advantage could be taken of these at sung celebrations or said; on 'high' days or 'low', either to introduce variety or to give a particular emphasis to a particular feast.

2   Using this Book with the ASB

ASB rubrics This book is designed for use, in the first instance, in conjunction with the ASB 1980. Accordingly all the rules, notes and rubrics to that book should be observed as far as possible. The aim has been chiefly to supplement rather than alter. Where alterations have been suggested a full explanation has been given. Both the canticles and intercessions that this book offers have been selected for the most appropriate days and seasons as far as possible, but there is nothing to prevent users from making different choices from this selection if it suits their purpose better, or exchanging morning for evening material, especially where only one service is being held in the day.

The opening responses Historically these were different at Morning Prayer from other Hours, but in the Prayer Book the morning responses, *O Lord, open thou our lips*, etc., were combined with the evening ones, *O God, make speed to save us*, etc. The ASB retains the Cranmer pattern for the first response but innovates for the second with, *Let us worship the Lord*, etc. The new Orders in the Anglican Provinces in the USA and Canada have retained the traditional pattern and it is hard to see why ASB made the change. There may be those who would wish to retain *O Lord, open*, etc. for the morning and *O God, make speed*, etc. for the evening.

Gloria Patri* and *Alleluia Cranmer deleted the *Alleluia* following the *Gloria Patri* and substituted, *Praise ye the Lord*, etc. This is only faintly recognizable in ASB in the response before the *Gloria Patri*, *All praise to his name*, and *Praise ye the Lord* has disappeared. Again, following America and Canada, we might do well to reinstate the *Alleluia* as they have done, which would not only restore a link with tradition but also forge a link with sister provinces. *Alleluia* is normally omitted in Lent, and *then* there might be a case for using *Let us worship the Lord*, etc., following the old Latin liturgy's *Gloria tibi, Domine* in Lent.

Invitatory Psalm (*Venite*, etc.) It will be seen that the selection of Invitatory psalms in ASB has been widened in this book to include Psalms 24, 67 and 95 *in full*. Suggested seasons for using these will be found in Appendix 2. The purpose of the Invitatory is to invite the participants to begin the *whole day* with prayer. It originated in the monastic Hour of Mattins, and is only 'tacked on' to Morning Prayer (Lauds) for the benefit of those who do not attend that Hour. In some sense it is distinct from Morning Prayer. The use of Psalm 134 to begin Evening Prayer, therefore, is to misunderstand the meaning of the Invitatory, and could only be justified if that were to begin the first Evensong of a major festival. On that basis it would be logical to omit it from the Morning Prayer following (ASB p. 27, rule 5). The *Phos Hilaron*, on the other hand, has a long history as an evening Office hymn and should not be confused as an Invitatory as ASB seems to do. The Office hymn comes most conveniently before the psalms of the day in order to draw the worshippers firmly into the celebration.

Psalmody At the heart of the Office lies the praise of God; indeed that is its chief function. The revised *cursus* of the ASB ensures that this never becomes burdensome. It may be, however, that some may wish to supplement the basic diet with such traditional seasonal psalms as the Penitential Psalms in Lent, the Psalms of Ascent in Advent, the *Hallel* Psalms in Eastertide and the *Laudate* Psalms on Sunday mornings. In such a case *one* psalm from those groups should be said *before* the psalms of the day. These psalms are listed in Appendix 3.

The Doxology It is usual to conclude each psalm and canticle with the doxology, *Gloria Patri*, but others are available, such as the verse which concludes Psalm 72. A doxology such as this might be an appropriate conclusion to the OT canticles. In some canticles a doxology is an integral part of the text, in which case the *Gloria Patri* is omitted. These self-contained doxologies will appear in the text in **bold type**. There is a long tradition of omitting the *Gloria Patri* from all psalms and canticles at all Hours on Maundy Thursday,

Good Friday and Easter Eve. At an Office of the Dead, the *Rest eternal* may be substituted for the usual doxology (see notes on relevant canticles).

Readings These should be used according to the ASB lectionary in the normal way, though suffice it to say that historically the emphasis in the Office was heavily on the worship of God and only in the monastic Hour of Mattins did scriptural reading find any great place. In the Church of England we have inherited to a large extent a solid diet of reading stemming from the Reformation principle of edification, justifiable in its day, perhaps, when books and other aids to Bible study were a rarity. Now that the ASB also has a daily eucharistic lectionary, the diet becomes heavy indeed for anyone partaking of that as well. Surely this is due for review. After saying all that, it may seem churlish to suggest that there ought to be room in the Office for a daily reading from a patristic lectionary; for suggestions, please see Appendix 4.

Canticles Notes on the position of the canticles and their recitation follow in sections 3 and 4 of this Introduction, below. For the moment, it must be stressed that the Gospel canticles have a special status in the Office as an evangelical climax to the worship. The Liturgy of Time has always required a sense of chronology in its structure, so that the hopes and promises of the OT may be articulated in the NT, and in the Gospel above all. Accordingly the arrangement of the canticles in this book for morning and evening bears this out, and in each case they are recited *before* the Gospel canticles. There are one or two exceptions to this general rule, and indeed, some canticles are a composition of OT and NT texts while others are not strictly biblical at all, such as *Jesus, Saviour of the world*, found in ASB. Some may wish to take a different view of the significance of the Gospel canticle and argue that it forms a pivot where the Office turns to its climax in the *reading* from the Gospel that follows. If this view were held, it could affect the position chosen for the Gospel canticle in the structure of the Office. Against this it has to be pointed out that such an interpretation only holds good where a reading from the

Gospel does actually follow the Gospel canticle, and *historically* there have never been Gospel readings in the Office. Such an interpretation is peculiarly Anglican and indeed recent, for only recently has the *Benedictus* preceded the second reading, a position long held by the *Te Deum*. The Gospel canticles are not reproduced in this book.

So far, nothing has been said in this Introduction about music. Needless to say, canticles are intended to be sung. While no attempt has been made to offer tones or chants for the canticles here, some care has been taken to ensure that they are all singable. Suggestions for sources of such music will be found in Appendix 1.

Two further canticles merit comment at this stage, the *Gloria in excelsis* and the *Nunc Dimittis*. The *Gloria* traditionally was a canticle that ended the Eastern Rite morning Office of *Orthros* from whence it became attracted to the beginning of the Eucharist, where today in the West it is most usually found. It seems unnecessary to use the *Gloria* as an Office canticle as frequently as the ASB scheme suggests, especially when so many other canticles are to be had. However, there would be an appropriateness in using (singing!) the *Gloria* at Morning Prayer in the Christmas season when a daily Eucharist is not provided.

After many years of unofficial use, the Church of England now has an official order for Compline, or Night Prayer. It is to this Office that the *Nunc Dimittis* properly belongs. There seems little point in reciting it at Evening Prayer when Night Prayer is said so widely. In any case at Evening Prayer it is not obligatory, and so alternatives may be used, and appropriately so when a baptism takes place at Evening Prayer (see Table of Canticles). Notes on the position to be given to the *Nunc Dimittis* if it is used at Evening Prayer follow below. Care should also be taken regarding its use on the feast of the Presentation of Christ in the Temple, when its correct place is in the eucharistic liturgy.

Suffrages The suffrages and collects of the ASB have largely been inherited from the BCP with little change. Our aim has been to enable set forms to vary with the season, at the same time providing a stimulus to prayer of intercession while making the structure more free. For this reason, when using the intercessions offered in this book there ought to be room for (1) free prayer by all present between the set form and the collects that follow, and (2) silent prayer. If a collect for a special subject is chosen it would be better used to round off a period of free prayer before proceeding with the rest of the Office, than to add it after the 'third collect'.

Most of the intercessions in this book have a three-part structure to each suffrage. The first two parts are divided by a colon. In small groups of worshippers where all will have a copy the first section could be said by the leader and the second by all, and the third part, the repeating response, omitted. In larger groups it may be simpler to let the leader take the first two parts and leave the third, the repeating response, to the people. The intercessions may be chanted to great effect, and in this method the people might follow each suffrage made by the leader with a repeating *Kyrie eleison* such as is found in the Taizé publications.

Silence This important part of prayer should never be overlooked by anyone leading the Office. Appropriate places for silence will be as recommended by the rubrics of ASB, for instance after readings. Other points might come before the act of confession and at the end of each psalm and canticle (where anciently also followed a collect; modern versions of these are available). As mentioned above there should be time for silence during the intercessions.

Collects The collect for the Day as well as for the Hour should not be omitted. The collects indicate clearly that the Office is the Liturgy of Time, and should help to draw the worshipper into the mystery of the Season or Feast (the time of year), as well as articulating the time of day. The Eucharist, by contrast, can be celebrated at any hour and so has no collect of the Hour; indeed, the Eucharist is the liturgy that transcends time.

The Ending The Office may be fitly ended with material found on p. 107 of ASB; first the greeting (para. 17) and the Grace said by all (para. 15).

3   The Position of Canticles and Intercessions

As already pointed out, the proper place for canticles is with the psalmody, leaving the Gospel canticles to stand in a place of emphasis on their own. The OT canticles ought therefore to come immediately after the psalms and before the first reading at Morning Prayer, and the NT canticles in the corresponding place at Evening Prayer. The *Benedictus* and *Magnificat* should retain their places after the first reading according to the rubrics, and the alternative canticles that follow the second reading *should then be omitted* (method 1, below). The Office should then continue with the sermon if any, or the Creed. If Night Prayer is not said and it is decided to say the *Nunc Dimittis* at Evening Prayer, this of course could follow the second reading in the normal way, but alternative canticles should not be used *at this point*.

METHOD 1	METHOD 2
Psalms	Psalms
OT/NT CANTICLE	
First Reading	First Reading
Benedictus/Magnificat	OT/NT CANTICLE
Second Reading	Second Reading
Canticle omitted (but *Nunc Dimittis* allowable at Evening Prayer)	*Benedictus/Magnificat*
(sermon)	(sermon)
Creed	Creed

An alternative to method 1, above, might be to use the alternative canticle after the first reading and the *Benedictus/Magnificat* after the second, leaving the psalmody untouched. If this method were used (method 2) it would not be possible to accommodate the *Nunc Dimittis* at Evening Prayer, and method 1, above, should be adopted.

Morning and Evening Prayer, Shorter Form
In the Shorter Forms, the rubrics provide one occasion only for canticles. We have already seen the importance of not omitting the Gospel canticles from the office, so where

should alternative canticles be fitted into this version of the Office? As they belong to the psalmody there should be no difficulty in following method 1 or method 2, above, at *Morning Prayer*, provided the appropriate canticle is inserted *between* the two readings. At Evening Prayer, where there is only one reading, method 1 will work, with the *Magnificat* being followed directly by the Lord's Prayer, and the *Nunc Dimittis* omitted. If, on the other hand, a reading from the patristic lectionary were put after the scriptural reading (as suggested elsewhere in this Introduction), then method 2 would work. Again, if the *Nunc Dimittis* were required, that could be accommodated still using method 1, but it would need to follow a second reading.

A note on the position of the intercessions
The intercessions should either precede or follow the Lord's Prayer at Morning and Evening Prayer, and the suffrages set should *not* be used; they are not in any case obligatory. Any biddings, extempore prayer or silent prayer should be added at this point, and not relegated to a place after the collects, for reasons given elsewhere.

In shorter forms, where no set suffrages are offered the alternative intercessions can conveniently be placed after the Lord's Prayer as in the standard version, but could just as appropriately precede the Lord's Prayer, which would then become a kind of common collect summing up the prayer by all.

4   A Note on the Recitation of Psalms and Canticles

The variety that the canticles bring to the Office is not only one of content, for their verse forms do not necessarily resemble those of the psalms. In many cases it will appear that the canticle verses are longer than psalm verses, and have their own rhythm which must be discovered and made apparent in recitation, and which could render them more suitable candidates for double chant than the psalms. Care should be taken, then, to recite the canticles in the same deliberate and unhurried manner as the psalms, and to observe a proper pause at the colon which divides each verse.

Apart from this colon there has been no attempt to supply any other form of musical pointing for the canticles in this book, which will of course vary with the setting chosen. The importance of this pause cannot be too highly stressed, for apart from giving time for drawing breath, it is an essential part of the rhythmic structure of any kind of communal recitation; even the breakers on the shore seem to hold back until just the right moment to crash. The pause is also a most useful mechanism for preventing communal recitation from becoming ragged, particularly if numbers attending are large. And as if all this were not reason enough, the pause provides a refreshing moment of reflection, an instant of prayer, without which the whole exercise would be in vain, and to which the whole purpose is directed.

Antiphonal or responsorial/antiphonal recitation, divided between two sides of a choir or between the officiant and the people, is probably the most usual form, though less ancient than responsorial, a form which lends itself to a situation where few have books or copies. Responsorial recitation has enjoyed a resurgence lately with such things as Gradual Psalms at the Eucharist, and commends itself where the amount of liturgical books and paper threatens to become a burden, and so detract from worship. Responsorial recitation can also be a very effective way of introducing variety, and a responsorial canticle between two antiphonal psalms works very well and might cause worshippers to rethink the position of the canticle accordingly. In the Roman rite the morning canticle is always placed between the psalms, but not for this reason! Accordingly, all the canticles in this book are given one or more responses for the people, which should be used before the first verse, after each *R* and after the doxology. Where there is more than one response the occasion of its proper use is indicated, and serves to emphasize the theme of the celebration for which the canticle is to be used.

The officiant should lead the people by beginning the response for the first time (before the first verse). He may wish to retain the pause at the colon in each verse, or he may wish to pause there only briefly, reserving the major pause *between* the verses where the response is not made.

In three cases (*Benedicite*, 'Bless the Lord' and Good Friday

Anthem 1) the response is 'built in' to the canticle, but this should not present any difficulty in recitation.

Neither the *Prayer Book* nor ASB has made provision for antiphons as a general feature of psalmody, but the congregational response provided for the canticles here could serve this additional purpose, if so desired, and also bring another element of variety to the totality of worship. In those circumstances the response is simply said by all, once before and after the canticle, and the verses recited antiphonally, as described above. The purpose of an antiphon is to sum up the theme of the psalm or canticle, and so lead the worshipper to prayer and contemplation. An antiphon also acts as a useful 'distance-piece' between separate psalms and canticles.

A final word about music. If set chants are felt to be too difficult to attempt, there is that well tried and very prayerful practice of intoning psalms and canticles on a single note, which adds dignity to the worship with simplicity.

5 A Note on the REB Translation

A high proportion of the canticles in this book are taken from the Revised English Bible, successor to the New English Bible, but the canticles themselves have been researched from such books as the *Canadian Book of Alternative Services*, the *Daily Office Revised* of the Joint Liturgical Group, the Franciscan Office Book and the Liturgy of the Hours, where they appear in different translations and sometimes in slightly different arrangements.

The REB is, of course, an untried version of Scripture, but its choice is not only an act of faith in the translator's art, but also the adoption of a version designed for recitation out loud, which commends itself for our present purpose. It also makes a general rule of using inclusive language. Every effort has been made not to alter the text and this has been done only where the constraints of liturgical recitation have made it necessary, and then most sparingly. In some instances a phrase has been omitted from a section, where to do so aids the division of verses for recitation without losing anything from the content. Where this happens it is usually obvious from the references given at the heading of each canticle. In a

number of cases a phrase has been abstracted from the text to
create a congregational response. Punctuation has been
simplified in places.

John Michael Mountney
St John the Baptist tide, 1989
Norwich

A Table of Canticles and Intercessions to be used throughout the year

Day/Season	Morning		Evening	
	CANTICLE	INTERCESSION	CANTICLE	INTERCESSION
SUNDAY (except Advent and Lent)	1	1a	46	1b
MONDAY	2	2a	47	2b
TUESDAY	3	3a	48	3b
WEDNESDAY	4	4a	49	4b
THURSDAY	5	5a	50	5b
FRIDAY	6	6a	51	6b
SATURDAY	7	7a	52	7b
SUNDAYS 3rd before Advent to Advent 4 (note e)	8	8a (see note c)	53	8b (see note c)
WEEKDAYS day after 3rd before Advent to day before Advent 1	9	8a	54	8b
WEEKDAYS day after Advent 1 to December 16	10	9a	55	9b
WEEKDAYS December 17 to 24	11	10a	56	10b, 10c (note d)
CHRISTMAS DAY	1	11a	57	11b
December 26–31	1/12	11a	57	11b
NAMING OF JESUS	1/13	12a	52	12b

Day/Season	Morning		Evening	
	CANTICLE	INTERCESSION	CANTICLE	INTERCESSION
January 2–5	13	12a	52	12b
EPIPHANY	1/14	13a	58	13b
January 7–12 (or day before Epiphany 1)	14	13a	58	13b
EPIPHANY 1	1/14	13a	58	13b
ASH WEDNESDAY to day before Lent 1	15/16 (note a)/ 17 (note b)	14a	59	14b
SUNDAYS in Lent	18	(see note c)	59	(see note c)
WEEKDAYS day after Lent 1 to day before Lent 3	19	14a	60	14b
WEEKDAYS day after Lent 3 to day before Lent 5	20	15a	61	15b
WEEKDAYS day after Lent 5 to Wednesday in Holy Week	21	16a	62	16b
MAUNDY THURSDAY	22	17a	63/50	17b
GOOD FRIDAY	23	18a	64	18b
EASTER EVE	24/6	19a	65	19b
EASTER DAY and SUNDAYS of EASTER-TIDE, WEEK-DAYS until day before EASTER 1	1	20a/21a	66/67	20b/21b

Day/Season	Morning		Evening	
	CANTICLE	INTERCESSION	CANTICLE	INTERCESSION
WEEKDAYS day after Easter 1 to day before Ascension	25/26	20a/21a	66/67	20b/21b
ASCENSION DAY (note f)	1	22a	58/52	22b
WEEKDAYS after Ascension to day before Pentecost	27	23a	68	23b
PENTECOST	1/27	24a	68	24b
TRINITY SUNDAY	1	25a	46	25b
TIMOTHY AND TITUS	28	37a	72	37b
CONVERSION ST PAUL	36	35a	70	35b
PRESENTATION OF CHRIST	13	26a	49	26b
ST JOSEPH	28	27a	57	27b
ANNUNCIATION	13	28a	57	28b
VISIT OF MARY	29	28a	69	28b
JOHN THE BAPTIST (both feasts)	30	29a	70	29b
MARY MAGDALEN	31	39a	69	39b
TRANS-FIGURATION	32	30a	58	30b
BLESSED VIRGIN MARY, Conception, Nativity, Falling Asleep	33	31a	47	31b
HOLY CROSS DAY	34	18a	62/48/52	18b

Day/Season	Morning		Evening	
	CANTICLE	INTERCESSION	CANTICLE	INTERCESSION
MICHAELMAS	1	32a	58	32b
ALL SAINTS	1	33a	70	33b
ALL SOULS	35	34a	71	34b
CHRIST THE KING	2/7	22c	58/53	22b
APOSTLES and EVANGELISTS	36	35a	70	35a
MARTYRS	35	36a	70	36b
TEACHERS	37	37a	72	37b
BISHOPS	28	37a	72	37b
ABBOTS and ABBESSES	38	37a	72	37b
MISSIONARIES	39	35b	72	35b
MYSTICS	40	38a	69	38b
ANY SAINT	32	33a	72	33b
WOMEN SAINTS	41/42	39a	69/42	39b
EMBERTIDE	43	40a	62	40b
HARVEST THANKS-GIVING	18	41a	18	41b
CHRISTIAN UNITY	44	42a/45a	63/50	42b/45b
GUIDANCE OF THE HOLY SPIRIT	27	23a	68	23b
BAPTISM AND CONFIRMA-TION	25/27	20a/21a/24a	66/67/68/47	20b/21b/24b
THANKSGIVING FOR HOLY COMMUNION	1	43a	46	43b
SOCIAL RESPON-SIBILITY	4	44a	51	44b

Day/Season	Morning		Evening	
	CANTICLE	INTERCESSION	CANTICLE	INTERCESSION
DEDICATION FESTIVAL/ CONSECRA- TION OF A CHURCH	45	45a	48/49	45b
REMEMBRANCE/ FUNERALS	35	34a/34b	71	34a/34b

a   If Penitential Order A is not used
b   If not used as a Lection
c   Sunday intercessions at these seasons follow those set for weekdays
d   Intercession 10c is supplied for Christmas Eve only
e   On the Sunday next before Advent may be celebrated Christ the King, q.v.
f   Sunday after Ascension Day as Ascension Day

The Canticles

Notes

The designations of the seasons are inclusive, e.g. 'Epiphany to Epiphany 1' means including Epiphany and Epiphany 1. The same applies to the intercessions.

Verses in square brackets [ ] may be omitted

A final verse printed in bold type indicates an inclusive doxology and the *Gloria Patri* is omitted.

This alternative doxology from Ps 72 may lend itself for use with OT canticles:

Blessed be his glorious name for ever: and let the whole earth be filled with his glory, Amen, Amen.

The two sets of canticles and intercessions for Eastertide to Ascension may be alternated at the will of the officiant by the week or the day. When these are used for baptism or confirmation they need not be applied strictly to their morning or evening positions, with the exception of Intercession 24b.

NEH = *New English Hymnal*

SUNDAY (except Third before Advent
to Advent 4 and Sundays in Lent)
CHRISTMAS DAY to NAMING
OF JESUS • EPIPHANY • EASTER WEEK
ASCENSION • PENTECOST • TRINITY
SUNDAY • MICHAELMAS
ALL SAINTS • THANKSGIVING FOR
HOLY COMMUNION
Morning

1 *Te Deum* (Parts 1 and 2)

R* **The Holy Church throughout the world acclaims the Lord.**

You are God and we praise you :
   you are the Lord and we acclaim you;

you are the eternal Father :
   all creation worships you.   *R*

To you all angels, all the powers of heaven :
   cherubim and seraphim sing in endless praise,

Holy holy holy Lord, God of power and might :
   heaven and earth are full of your glory.   *R*

The glorious company of apostles praise you :
   the noble fellowship of prophets praise you,
   the white-robed army of martyrs praise you.

Throughout the world the holy Church acclaims you :
   Father of majesty unbounded;   *R*

your true and only Son, worthy of all worship :
   and the Holy Spirit, advocate and guide.

You Christ are the King of glory :
   the eternal Son of the Father.   *R*

When you became man to set us free :
   you did not abhor the Virgin's womb.

You overcame the sting of death :
   and opened the kingdom of heaven to all believers.   *R*

You are seated at God's right hand in glory :
  we believe that you will come and be our judge.

Come then Lord and help your people :
  bought with the price of your own blood;   *R*

and bring us with your saints :
  to glory everlasting.   *R*

ASB

(Doxology not normally used with this canticle)

*Alternatives:
CHRISTMAS etc. *R* **You became a man to set us free.**
EPIPHANY *R* **You alone are worthy of all worship.**
EASTER *R* **You have overcome the sting of death, Alleluia.**
ASCENSION *R* **You, Christ, are the king of glory.**
PENTECOST *R* **We acclaim the Holy Spirit, advocate and
    guide.**
MICHAELMAS *R* **To you all angels sing in endless praise.**
ALL SAINTS *R* **Bring us with your saints to glory everlasting.**

MONDAY • CHRIST THE KING
Morning

2 ***The Song of David***   *I Chron 29.10–13*

R* **The Lord is exalted as head over all.**

Blessed are you, Lord God of our Father Israel : from of old and for ever.

Yours, Lord, is the greatness and the power : the glory, the splendour and the majesty.

For everything in heaven and on earth is yours : yours, Lord, is the sovereignty, and you are exalted over all as head.

Wealth and honour come from you : you rule over all.   *R*

Might and power are of your disposing : yours it is to give power and strength to all.

Now, our God, we give you thanks : and praise your glorious name.   *R*

REB

*Alternative for CHRIST THE KING:

R **Yours, Lord, is the majesty and the sovereignty.**

TUESDAY
Morning
3 *God the Victor* Isa 42.10–16a

R **Sing praise to the Lord throughout the world.**

Sing a new song to the Lord : sing his praise throughout the world.

You that sail the broad seas : and you that inhabit the coasts and islands. **R**

Let the wilderness and its settlements rejoice : and the encampments where Kedar lives.

Let the inhabitants of Sela shout for joy : let them cry out from the hilltops. **R**

Let the coasts and islands ascribe glory to the Lord : let them sing his praise.

The Lord will go forth as a warrior, a soldier roused to the fury of battle : he will shout, he will raise the battle cry and triumph over his foes. **R**

Long have I restrained myself : I kept silence and held myself in check.

Now I groan like a woman in labour : panting and gasping. **R**

I shall lay waste mountain and hill : and shrivel up all their herbage.

I shall change rivers into desert wastes : and dry up every pool. **R**

I shall lead the blind on their way : and guide them along paths they do not know.

I shall turn darkness into light before them : and make straight their twisting roads. **R**

REB

Morning

4   *The Poor Rejoice in the Lord*   *I Sam 2.1–10*

R*   **There is none so holy and righteous as the Lord.**

My heart exults in the Lord : in the Lord I hold my head high.

I gloat over my enemies : I rejoice because you have saved me.

There is none but you, none so holy as the Lord : none so righteous as our God.   *R*

Cease your proud boasting : let no word of arrogance pass your lips.

For the Lord is a God who knows : he governs what mortals do.

Strong men stand in mute dismay : but those who faltered put on new strength.   *R*

Those who had plenty, sell themselves for a crust : and the hungry grow strong again.

The barren woman bears seven children : and the mother of many sons is left to languish.   *R*

The Lord metes out both death and life : he sends down to Sheol, he can bring the dead up again.

Poverty and riches both come from the Lord : he brings low and he raises up.   *R*

He lifts the weak out of the dust : and raises the poor from the refuse heap

To give them a place among the great : to assign them seats of honour.   *R*

The foundations of the earth are the Lord's : and he has set the world upon them.

He will guard the footsteps of his loyal servants : while the wicked will be silenced in darkness, for it is not by strength that a mortal prevails.   *R*

Those who oppose the Lord will be terrified : when from heaven he thunders against them.

The Lord is judge : even to the ends of the earth.

He will endow his king with strength : and raise high the head of his anointed one.   *R*

REB

*Alternative for SOCIAL RESPONSIBILITY:

R   **The Lord raises the poor to give them a place of honour.**

THURSDAY
Morning

5   *Seek the Lord*   Isa 55.6–11

R   **The word of the Lord will succeed in its task.**

Seek the Lord while he is present : call to him while he is close at hand.

Let the wicked abandon their ways : and the evil their thoughts,   *R*

Let them return to the Lord who will take pity on them : and to our God, for he will freely forgive.

For my thoughts are not your thoughts : nor are your ways my ways.   *R*

But as the heavens are high above the earth : so are my ways high above your ways, and my thoughts above your thoughts.   *R*

As the rain and snow come down from the heavens : and do not return there without watering the earth,

Making it produce grain : to give seed for sowing and bread to eat.   *R*

So it is with my word, issuing from my mouth : it will not return to me empty

Without accomplishing my purpose : and succeeding in the task for which I sent it.   *R*

REB

Morning

6   *A Song of Anguish*   *Isa 38.10–14, 17–20*

R*   **Bitterness has been my lot, but your love has brought me joy.**

I said, in the prime of my life I must pass away : for the rest of my days I am consigned to the gates of Sheol.

I said, I shall no longer see the Lord : as I did in the land of the living. *R*

I shall no longer see my fellow men : as I did when I lived in the world.

My dwelling is taken from me : pulled up like a shepherd's tent. *R*

You have rolled up my life like a weaver : when he cuts the thread from the thrum.

Day and night you torment me : I am racked with pain till the morning. *R*

All my bones are broken, as if by a lion : day and night you torment me.

I twitter as if I were a swallow, I moan like a dove : my eyes are raised to heaven. *R*

Lord, pay heed, stand surety for me : bitterness, not prosperity would indeed be my lot.

But your love saved me from the pit of destruction : for you have thrust all my sins behind you. *R*

Sheol cannot confess you, Death cannot praise you : nor can those who go down to the abyss hope for your truth.

The living, only the living can confess you as I do this day, my God : just as a father makes your faithfulness known to his sons. *R*

The Lord is at hand to save me : so let the music of our
praises resound all our life long in the house of the Lord.   **R**

REB

*Alternative for EASTER EVE:

R   **Death cannot praise you, only the living can confess you.**

SATURDAY • CHRIST THE KING
Morning

7   ***Bless the Lord***   *Song of the Three 29–34*

Bless the Lord the God of our fathers :
   sing his praise and exalt him for ever.

Bless his holy and glorious name :
   sing his praise and exalt him for ever.

Bless him in his holy and glorious temple :
   sing his praise and exalt him for ever.

Bless him who beholds the depths :
   sing his praise and exalt him for ever.

Bless him who sits between the cherubim :
   sing his praise and exalt him for ever.

Bless him on the throne of his kingdom :
   sing his praise and exalt him for ever.

Bless him in the heights of heaven :
   sing his praise and exalt him for ever.

Bless the Father the Son and the Holy Spirit :
   sing his praise and exalt him for ever.

ASB

BEFORE ADVENT
SUNDAYS (Third before Advent to Advent 4)
Morning

8   *The Mountain of the Lord*   Isa 2.2–5

R   **Come, people of Jacob, let us walk in the light of the Lord.**

In the days to come the mountain of the Lord's house : will be set above all other mountains, raised high above the hills.

All the nations will stream towards it : and many peoples will go and say,   *R*

Let us go up to the mountain of the Lord : to the house of the God of Jacob

That he may teach us his ways : and that we may walk in his paths.   *R*

For instruction comes from Zion : and the word of the Lord from Jerusalem.

He will judge between the nations : as arbiter among many peoples.   *R*

They will beat their swords into mattocks : and their spears into pruning knives.

Nation will not lift sword against nation : nor ever again be trained for war.   *R*

REB

BEFORE ADVENT
WEEKDAYS (Monday after Third Sunday before Advent to day before Advent 1)
Morning

9   *God is my Salvation*   Isa 12.2–6

R   **With joy you will all draw water from the wells of deliverance.**

God is my deliverer : I am confident and unafraid

For the Lord is my refuge and defence : and has shown himself my deliverer.   *R*

On that day you will say : give thanks to the Lord, invoke him by name.

Make known among the peoples what he has done : proclaim that his name is exalted.   *R*

Sing psalms to the Lord for he has triumphed : let this be known in all the world.

Cry out, shout aloud, you dwellers in Zion : for the Holy One of Israel is among you in majesty.   *R*

REB

ADVENT
WEEKDAYS (day after Advent 1 to December 16)
Morning

10 **The Joy of Liberation**   *Jer 31.10–14*

R **The Lord has delivered Jacob from a foe too strong for him.**

Listen to the word of the Lord, you nations : announce it, make it known to coastlands far away.

He who scattered Israel will gather them again : and watch over them as a shepherd watches his flock.   *R*

They will come with shouts of joy to Zion's height : radiant at the bounty of the Lord,

The grain, the new wine and the oil : the young of flock and herd.   *R*

They will be like a well-watered garden : and never languish again.

Girls will then dance for joy : and men young and old will rejoice.   *R*

I shall turn their grief into gladness : comfort them, and give them joy after sorrow.

I shall satisfy the priests with the fat of the land : and my people will have their fill of my bounty.   *R*

REB

11 ***The People that Walked in Darkness***   *Isa 9.2–7*

R   **His title will be wonderful Counsellor, mighty Hero, Prince of peace.**

The people that walked in darkness has seen a great light : on those who lived in a land as dark as death a light has dawned.

You have increased their joy and given them great gladness : they rejoice in your presence as those who rejoice at harvest, as warriors rejoice when dividing the spoil.   **R**

For you have broken the yoke that burdened them, the rod laid on their shoulders : the driver's goad, as on the day of Midian's defeat.

The boots of earth-shaking armies on the march, the soldiers' cloaks rolled in blood : are all destined to be burnt, food for the fire.   **R**

For a child has been born to us, a son is given to us : he will bear the symbol of dominion on his shoulder.

Wide will be the dominion and boundless the peace : bestowed on David's throne and on his kingdom   **R**

To establish and support it : with justice and righteousness.

From now on, for evermore : the zeal of the Lord of Hosts will do this.   **R**

REB

CHRISTMAS to December 31 (if a Eucharist is not celebrated)
Morning

12 *Gloria in Excelsis*

R   **You alone are the Holy One,
 you alone are the Lord.**

Glory to God in the highest :
 and peace to his people on earth.   *R*

Lord God, heavenly King :
 almighty God and Father,

we worship you, we give you thanks :
 we praise you for your glory.   *R*

Lord Jesus Christ, only Son of the Father :
 Lord God, Lamb of God,

you take away the sin of the world :
 have mercy on us;   *R*

you are seated at the right hand of the Father :
 receive our prayer.

For you alone are the Holy One :
 you alone are the Lord,

you alone are the Most High,
 Jesus Christ, with the Holy Spirit :
 in the glory of God the Father. Amen.   *R*

ASB

(Doxology omitted)

NAMING OF JESUS to January 5 (but not on intervening Sunday)
PRESENTATION OF CHRIST
ANNUNCIATION
Morning

13   *The New Jerusalem*   *Isa 60.1–3, 11, 14, 18, 19*

R   **Arise, shine, Jerusalem, for your light has come.**

Arise, shine, Jerusalem, for your light has come : and over you the glory of the Lord has dawned.   *R*

Though darkness covers the earth and dark night the nations : on you the Lord shines and over you his glory will appear.

Nations will journey towards your light : and kings to your radiance.   *R*

Your gates will stand open at all times : day and night they will never be shut.

All who reviled you will address you as City of the Lord : Zion of the Holy One of Israel.   *R*

No longer will the sound of violence be heard in your land : nor havoc and ruin within your borders

But you will name your walls Deliverance : and your gates Praise.   *R*

The sun will no longer be your light by day : nor the moon shine on you by night.

The Lord will be your everlasting light : your God will be your splendour.   *R*

REB

Morning

14 *Many Nations*   *Tob 13.7–11, 13–15*

R   **My soul, praise the Lord, the great King.**

I shall exalt my God and rejoice in the King of Heaven : let all men tell of his majesty and in Jerusalem give him thanks.

O Jerusalem, Holy City, he will punish you for what your sons have done : but he will have mercy once more on the righteous.   *R*

Give thanks to the Lord for his goodness, and praise to the eternal King : your sanctuary will be rebuilt for you with rejoicing.

May he give happiness to all your exiles : and cherish for all generations those in distress.   *R*

Your radiance will shine to the ends of the earth : many nations will come to you from afar

To your holy name from every corner of the earth : bearing gifts in their hands for the King of heaven.   *R*

In you endless generations will utter their joy : the name of the chosen city will endure for ever.

Come then, be joyful for the righteous, for they will be gathered together : and will praise the eternal Lord.   *R*

How happy will they be who love you : and happy those who rejoice in your prosperity.

Happy those who grieve for you in all your afflictions : they will rejoice over you and behold all your joy for ever.   *R*

REB

15 *The Prayer of Azariah*   *Song of the Three 3–7, 11–18*

R   **For the sake of your honour, do not abandon us for ever.**

Blessed are you and worthy of praise, Lord, the God of our fathers : your name is glorious for ever.

You are just in all you have done to us, all your works are true : your paths are straight, your judgements all true.   *R*

Just is the sentence in all that you have brought upon us, and on Jerusalem, the holy city of our ancestors : true and just the sentence you have passed upon our sins.

For we sinned and broke your law in rebellion against you : in all we did, we sinned.   *R*

Do not withdraw your mercy from us, for the sake of Abraham your friend : for the sake of Isaac your servant and Israel your holy one.

You promised them that their descendants should be as numerous as the stars in the sky : as the grains of sand on the seashore.   *R*

Yet, Lord, we have been made the smallest of all nations : for our sins we are today the most abject in the world.

Now we have no ruler, no prophet, no leader : there is no whole-offering, no sacrifice, no oblation, no incense, no place to make an offering before you and find mercy.   *R*

But we come with contrite heart and humbled spirit : may we be accepted

As though we came with whole offerings of rams and bullocks and with thousands of fat lambs : let our sacrifice be made before you this day.   *R*

That we may obey you in everything : for no shame shall come to those who put their trust in you.

Now we shall follow you with our whole heart : and in fear seek your presence.   *R*

REB

ASH WEDNESDAY to day before Lent 1
(Alternative if Penitential Order A not used)
Morning

16 *A Canticle of Repentance* *Prayer of Manasseh 1a, 2, 4, 6, 7, 9b–14*

R **Lord, hear us : Lord, have mercy.**

Lord almighty, God of our fathers :
 maker of highest heaven and the manifold order of earth;

All things are filled with awe and tremble at your power :
 yet infinite and unsearchable is your merciful promise. *R*

You are the Lord most high
  full of compassion, patience and mercy :
 you are moved when your children suffer for their sins.

In your goodness, Lord, you have promised
  forgiveness to those who sin against you :
 in your boundless mercy you have appointed
  repentance as the way to salvation. *R*

By reason of my offences :
 I am not worthy to look up
  and behold the heights of heaven.

Now therefore do I bow the knees of my heart :
 and ask for your forgiveness. *R*

I have sinned, Lord, I have sinned :
 I acknowledge my transgression.

I humbly pray, Spare me, Lord, spare me :
 do not be angry with me for ever. *R*

Deliver me from evil :
 do not abandon me to the grave.

For you, Lord, are the God of the penitent :
 in me you will show forth all your goodness. *R*

Unworthy though I am
  you will save me in your mercy :
 and I will praise you continually
  all the days of my life.

For all the powers of heaven sing your praise :
 yours are the kingdom and the glory. *R*

Lent, Holy Week and Easter

ASH WEDNESDAY to day before Lent 1
(Alternative if not used as a lection)
Morning

17 ***A Song of Hosea***   *Hosea 6.1–6*

R   **Come, let us return to the Lord.**

He has torn us, but he will heal us : he has wounded us, but he will bind up our wounds.

After two days he will revive us : on the third day he will raise us to live in his presence.   *R*

Let us strive to know the Lord : whose coming is as sure as the sunrise.

He will come to us like the rain : like spring rains that water the earth.   *R*

How shall I deal with you, Ephraim : how shall I deal with you, Judah?

Your loyalty to me is like the morning mist : like dew that vanishes early.   *R*

That is why I have cut them to pieces by the prophets : and slaughtered them with my words, my judgment goes forth like light.

For I require loyalty, not sacrifice : acknowledgement of God rather than whole-offerings.   *R*

REB

LENT SUNDAYS
Morning
HARVEST THANKSGIVING
Morning or Evening

18   *A Song of Creation*   Song of the Three 35–68

*Bless the Lord all created things :
  sing his praise and exalt him for ever.

*Bless the Lord you heavens :
  sing his praise and exalt him for ever.

*Bless the Lord you angels of the Lord :
  bless the Lord of you his hosts;

Bless the Lord you waters above the heavens :
  sing his praise and exalt him for ever.

Bless the Lord sun and moon :
  bless the Lord you stars of heaven;

bless the Lord all rain and dew :
  sing his praise and exalt him for ever.

Bless the Lord all winds that blow :
  bless the Lord you fire and heat;

bless the Lord scorching wind and bitter cold :
  sing his praise and exalt him for ever.

Bless the Lord dews and falling snows :
  bless the Lord you nights and days;

bless the Lord light and darkness :
  sing his praise and exalt him for ever.

Bless the Lord frost and cold :
  bless the Lord you ice and snow;

bless the Lord lightnings and clouds :
  sing his praise and exalt him for ever.

O let the earth bless the Lord :
  bless the Lord you mountains and hills;

bless the Lord all that grows in the ground :
  sing his praise and exalt him for ever.

Bless the Lord you springs :
  bless the Lord you seas and rivers;

Cont.

bless the Lord you whales and all that swim in the waters :
    sing his praise and exalt him for ever.

Bless the Lord all birds of the air :
    bless the Lord you beasts and cattle;

*bless the Lord all men on the earth :
    sing his praise and exalt him for ever.

*O People of God bless the Lord :
    bless the Lord you priests of the Lord;

*bless the Lord you servants of the Lord :
    sing his praise and exalt him for ever.

*Bless the Lord all men of upright spirit :
    bless the Lord you that are holy and humble in heart.

*Bless the Father, the Son and the Holy Spirit :
    sing his praise and exalt him for ever.

ASB

* Indicates verses used in its shortened form in ASB

LENT

WEEKDAYS (day after Lent 1 to day before
Lent 3)

Morning

19 ***A Lament*** *Jer 14.17–21*

R **Lord, we have sinned against you.**

Let my eyes stream with tears : night and day without
ceasing,

For the virgin daughter of my people struck by a cruel blow :
is grievously wounded. *R*

If I go out into the open country : I see those slain by the
sword.

If I enter the city : I see the victims of famine. *R*

Prophet and priest alike wander : without rest in the land.

Have you spurned Judah utterly, do you loathe Zion : why
have you wounded us past all healing? *R*

We hoped to prosper, but nothing went well : we hoped for
respite, but terror struck.

We acknowledge our wickedness, the guilt of our
forefathers : Lord we have sinned against you. *R*

Do not despise the place where your name dwells : or bring
contempt on your glorious throne.

Remember your covenant with us : and do not make
it void. *R*

REB

LENT

WEEKDAYS (day after Lent 3 to day before
Lent 5)

Morning

20 *The Judgement of God*   Hab 3.2–4, 13a, 15, 16a, 17–19

R   **The Lord God is my strength.**

Lord, I have heard of your fame : Lord, I am in awe of what
you have done.

Through all generations you have made yourself known :
and in your wrath you did not forget your mercy.   *R*

God comes from Teman : the Holy One from Mount Paran.

His radiance covers the sky : and his splendour fills
the earth.   *R*

His brightness is like the dawn, rays of light flash from his
hand : and thereby his might is veiled.

You go forth to save your people : to save your
anointed one.   *R*

When you tread the sea with your steeds : the mighty waters
foam.

I hear, and my body quakes : my lips quiver at
the sound.   *R*

Weakness overcomes my limbs : my feet totter in their
tracks.

The fig tree has no buds : the vines bear no harvest.   *R*

The olive crop fails : the orchards yield no food.

The fold is bereft of its flock : and there are no cattle in
the stalls.   *R*

Even so I exult in the Lord : and rejoice in the God who
saves me.

He makes me as sure-footed as a hind : and sets my feet on
the heights.   *R*

REB

LENT

WEEKDAYS (day after Lent 5 to Wednesday in Holy Week)

Morning

21 *The Suffering Servant*   Isa 53.2–6

R   **He became for us the man of sorrows.**

He grew up before the Lord like a young plant : whose roots are in parched ground.

He had no beauty, no majesty to catch our eyes : no grace to attract us to him.   **R**

He was despised, shunned by all : pain-racked and afflicted by disease.

We despised him, we held him of no account : an object from which people turn their eyes.   **R**

Yet it was our afflictions he was bearing : our pain he endured,

While we thought of him as smitten by God : struck down by disease and misery.   **R**

But he was pierced for our transgressions : crushed for our iniquities.

The chastisement he bore restored us to health : and by his wounds we are healed.   **R**

We had all strayed like sheep : each of us going his own way.

But the Lord laid on him : the guilt of us all.   **R**

REB

MAUNDY THURSDAY
Morning

22   *The First Lamentation*   *Lam 1.1–4*

R   **Jerusalem, Jerusalem, turn again to the Lord, your God.**

How deserted lies the city once thronging with people : once great among nations, now become a widow.   *R*

Once queen among the provinces, now put to forced labour : she weeps bitterly in the night, tears run down her cheeks.   *R*

Among all who loved her she has no one to bring her comfort : her friends have all betrayed her, they have become her enemies.   *R*

Judah has wasted away through affliction and endless servitude : living among the nations, she has found no resting-place.   *R*

Her persecutors all fell on her in her sore distress : the approaches to Zion mourn, for no pilgrims attend her sacred feasts.   *R*

All her gates are desolate, her priests groan : her maidens are made to suffer, how bitter is her fate.   *R*

REB

GOOD FRIDAY
Morning

23   *The Second Lamentation*   *Lam 3.19–30*

R   **Jerusalem, Jerusalem, turn again to the Lord, your God.**

The memory of my distress and my wanderings is wormwood and gall : I remember them indeed and am filled with despondency.   *R*

I shall wait patiently because I take this to heart : the Lord's love is surely not exhausted nor has his compassion failed.   *R*

They are new every morning, so great is his constancy : The Lord, I say, is all that I have, therefore I shall wait patiently for him.   *R*

The Lord is good to those who look to him, to anyone who seeks him : it is good to wait in patience for deliverance by the Lord.   *R*

It is good for a man to bear the yoke from youth : let him sit alone in silence if it is heavy on him.   *R*

Let him lie face downwards on the ground and there may yet be hope : let him offer his cheek to the smiter and endure full measure of abuse.   *R*

REB

EASTER EVE
Morning
24   *The Third Lamentation*   Lam 5.1–5, 7–10, 15

R   **Jerusalem, Jerusalem, turn again to the Lord, your God.**

Remember, Lord, what has befallen us, look and see how we are scorned : the land we possessed is turned over to strangers, our homes to foreigners.   *R*

We are like orphans without a father, our mothers are like widows : we have to buy water to drink, water which is ours, our wood can be had only for payment.   *R*

The yoke is on our necks, we are harassed, we are weary but allowed no rest : our forefathers sinned, now they are no more, and we must bear the burden of their guilt.   *R*

Slaves have become our rulers, and there is no one to free us from their power : we must bring in our food from the wilderness at the risk of our lives in the scorching heat.   *R*

Our skins are blackened as in a furnace by the ravages of starvation : joy has vanished from our hearts, our dancing is turned to mourning.   *R*

REB

EASTERTIDE (day after Easter 1 to day before Ascension – Alternative A)

BAPTISM • CONFIRMATION

Morning

25 *Let us sing to the Lord*   Exod 15.1–3, 6, 8–11, 13

R* **Sing to the Lord, for he has won a glorious victory.**

Let us sing to the Lord for he has won a glorious victory : the horse and its rider he has hurled into the sea.

The Lord is my strength and my song : he has become my salvation.   *R*

He is my God and I will praise him : my father's God and I will exalt him.

The Lord fights for his people : the Lord is his name.   *R*

Your right hand, Lord, is glorious in power : your right hand, Lord, shatters the enemy.

[At the blast of your anger the sea piled up : the water stood up like a bank.   *R*

The enemy boasted, I shall pursue : I shall overtake, I shall divide the spoil.

I shall glut my appetite on them, I shall draw my sword : I shall rid myself of them.   *R*

You blew with your blast, the sea covered them : they sank like lead in the swelling waves.]

Who is like you, Lord, majestic in holiness : who is like you, Lord, awesome in glory, working wonders?   *R*

In your unfailing love : you will lead the people you have redeemed.

And by your invincible strength : you will guide them to your holy dwelling.   *R*

Lent, Holy Week and Easter, expanded

*Alternative for BAPTISM and CONFIRMATION:

R **The Lord has become my salvation.**

EASTERTIDE (day after Easter 1 to day before Ascension – Alternative B)

Morning

26 ***Listen, O Heavens***   *Deut 32.1–10a, 13b, 14*

R   **I will proclaim the name of the Lord.**

Listen, O heavens and I will speak : hear, O earth the words of my mouth.

Let my teaching fall like rain and my words descend like dew : like fine rain on new grass and like showers on tender plants.   *R*

I will proclaim the name of the Lord : O praise the greatness of our God.

He is the creator, his works are perfect and all his ways are just : a faithful God who does no wrong, holy, righteous and true is he.   *R*

[Perverted and crooked generation : whose faults have proved you no children of his,

Is this how you repay the Lord : you senseless and stupid people?   *R*

Is he not your father who formed you : did he not make you and establish you?

Remember the days of old : think of the years, age upon age.   *R*

When the Most High gave each nation its heritage : when he divided all mankind

He laid down the boundaries for the peoples : according to the number of the sons of God.   *R*

But the Lord's share was his own people : Jacob was his allotted portion.

He found his people in a desert land : in a barren, howling waste.   *R*

He satisfied them with honey from the crags : and oil from the flinty rock,

With curds from the cattle and the finest flour of wheat : and you, his people, drank red wine from the juice of the grape.   *R*]

Lent, Holy Week and Easter, expanded

DAY AFTER ASCENSION TO PENTECOST
GUIDANCE OF THE HOLY SPIRIT
BAPTISM • CONFIRMATION
Morning

27 *New Life*   Ezek 36.24–28

R   **I will put a new spirit within you, says the Lord.**

I shall take you from among the nations, and gather you from every land : and bring you to your homeland.

I shall sprinkle pure water over you, and you will be purified from everything that defiles you : I shall purify you from the taint of all your idols.   *R*

I shall give you a new heart : and put a new spirit within you.

I shall remove the heart of stone from your body : and give you a heart of flesh.   *R*

I shall put my spirit within you and make you conform to my statutes : you will observe my laws faithfully.

Then you will live in the land I gave to your forefathers : you will be my people and I shall be your God.   *R*

REB

TIMOTHY AND TITUS • ST JOSEPH
BISHOPS
Morning

28 ***The Good Shepherd*** Isa 40.10–17

R **Like a shepherd he will tend his flock.**

Here is the Lord God, he is coming in might : coming to rule
with powerful arm.

His reward is with him : his recompense before him. *R*

Like a shepherd he will tend his flock : and with his arm keep
them together.

He will carry the lambs in his bosom : and lead the ewes
to water. *R*

Who has measured the waters of the sea in the hollow of his
hand : or with its span gauged the heavens?

Who has held all the soil of the earth in a bushel : or weighed
the mountains in a balance, the hills on a pair of scales? *R*

Who has directed the spirit of the Lord, what counsellor
stood at his side to instruct him : with whom did he confer to
gain discernment?

Who taught him this path of justice, or taught him
knowledge : or showed him the way of wisdom? *R*

To him the nations are but drops from a bucket : no more
than moisture on the scales.

To him coasts and islands weigh : as light as specks
of dust. *R*

Lebanon does not yield wood enough for fuel : beasts enough
for a whole-offering.

All the nations are as naught in his sight : he reckons them as
less than nothing. *R*

REB

VISIT OF MARY TO ELIZABETH
Morning

29 *The Song of the Herald* Isa 52.7–10, 1a

R How beautiful on the mountains is the herald of good news.

How beautiful on the mountains are the feet of the herald :
the bringer of good news

Announcing deliverance, proclaiming to Zion : Your God
has become King. *R*

Your watchmen raise their voices and shout together in joy :
for with their own eyes they see the Lord return to Zion.

Break forth together into shouts of joy, you ruins of
Jerusalem : for the Lord has comforted his people, he has
redeemed Jerusalem. *R*

The Lord has bared his holy arm in the sight of all nations :
and the whole world from end to end shall see the
deliverance wrought by our God.

Awake, awake, Zion, put on your strength : Jerusalem, Holy
City, put on your splendid garments. *R*

REB

JOHN THE BAPTIST (both feasts)
Morning

30 ***The Justice of God***   Isa 33.13–16

R   **The just will dwell on the heights.**

You dwellers afar off, hear what I have done : acknowledge
my might, you that are near at hand.

Sinners in Zion quake with terror : the godless are seized
with trembling.   *R*

They ask, Can any of us live with a devouring fire : can any
of us live in perpetual flames?

The person who behaves uprightly and speaks the truth :
who scorns to enrich himself by extortion.   *R*

Who keeps his hands clean from bribery, who stops his ears
against talk of murder : and closes his eyes against looking at
evil

He it is who will dwell on the heights, his refuge a fastness in
the cliffs : his food assured and water never failing him.   *R*

REB

MARY MAGDALEN
Morning

31 ***The Song of the Beloved***   Song of Songs 8.6–7

R   **Many waters cannot quench love.**

Wear me as a seal over your heart : as a seal upon your arm.

For love is strong as death : passion cruel as the grave.   *R*

It blazes up like a blazing fire : fiercer than any flame.

Many waters cannot quench love : no flood can sweep
it away.   *R*

If someone were to offer for love all the wealth in his house :
it would be laughed to scorn.   *R*

REB

TRANSFIGURATION • ANY SAINT
Morning

32　*A Song of the Bride*　Isa 61.10–11; 62.1–5

R*　**All nations shall see your glory and rejoice.**

Let me rejoice in the Lord with all my heart : let me exult in my God.

For he has robed me in deliverance and arrayed me in victory : like a bridegroom with his garland or a bride decked in her jewels.　*R*

As the earth puts forth her blossom : or plants in the garden burst into flower

So will the Lord God make his victory and renown : blossom before all the nations.　*R*

For Zion's sake I shall not keep silent, for Jerusalem's sake I shall not be quiet : until her victory shines forth like the sunrise, her deliverance like a blazing torch.

And the nations see your victory : and all the kings your glory.　*R*

Then you will be called by a new name : which the Lord himself will announce.

You will be a glorious crown in the Lord's hand : a royal diadem held by your God.　*R*

No more will you be called Forsaken, no more will your land be called Desolate : but you will be named Hephzibah and your land Beulah.

For the Lord will take delight in you : and to him your land will be linked in wedlock.　*R*

As a young man weds a maiden : so will you be wedded to him who rebuilds you.

And as a bridegroom rejoices over the bride : so will your God rejoice over you.　*R*

REB

*Alternative for ANY SAINT:
R　**The Lord will take delight in his bride.**

BLESSED VIRGIN MARY (CONCEPTION*)
NATIVITY (FALLING ASLEEP**)
Morning

33   *A Song of Consolation*   *Isa 66.10–14a*

R   **Rejoice with Jerusalem and find your comfort in her.**

Rejoice with Jerusalem and exult in her : all you that love her.

Share her joy with all your heart : all you that mourned over her.   *R*

Then you may suck comfort from her and be satisfied : taking with enjoyment her plentiful milk.

These are the words of the Lord, I shall make prosperity flow over her like a river : and the wealth of the nations like a stream in spate.   *R*

Her babes will be carried in her arms : and dandled on her knees.

As a mother comforts her son, so shall I myself comfort you : in Jerusalem you will find comfort.   *R*

At the sight your heart will be glad : you will flourish like grass in spring.

The Lord will make his power known : among his servants.   *R*

REB

* BCP Calendar December 8
** A common dedication of churches and found in Oxford
University Calendar, and calendars of other Anglican provinces,
August 15

HOLY CROSS DAY
Morning

34 *A Song of the Redeemer* Isa 63.1–3a, 7–9

R **We recount the Lord's unfailing love.**

Who is this coming from Edom, from Bozrah with his
garments stained red : one spendidly attired, striding along
with mighty power?

It is I, proclaiming victory : I, who am strong to save. *R*

Why are your clothes all red : like the garments of one
treading grapes in the winepress?

I have trodden the press alone : for none of my people was
with me. *R*

I shall recount the Lord's unfailing love : the prowess of the
Lord

According to all he has done for us : his great goodness to
the house of Israel. *R*

What he has done for them in his tenderness : and by his
many acts of faithful love.

He said, Surely they are my people, children who will not
play me false : and he became their deliverer in all
their troubles. *R*

No envoy, no angel, but he himself delivered them :
redeemed them in his love and pity.

He lifted them up and carried them : through all the days
of old. *R*

REB

Morning

35 *The Souls of the Righteous* *Wisd 3.1–8*

R **They will be like judges and rulers over all.**

The souls of the just are in God's hand : no torment will touch them.

In the eyes of the foolish they seemed to be dead : and their departure reckoned as defeat, and their going from us as disaster. *R*

But they are at peace, for though in the sight of men they may suffer punishment : they have a sure hope of immortality,

And after a little chastisement : they will receive great blessings. *R*

Because God has tested them and found them worthy to be his : he put them to the proof like gold in a crucible

And found them acceptable : like an offering burnt whole on the altar. *R*

In the hour of their judgement they will shine in glory : and will sweep over the world like sparks through stubble.

They will be judges and rulers over nations and peoples : and the Lord will be their king for ever. *R*

REB

* When used for Remembrance or Funerals, the *Gloria Patri* may be omitted and the following verse substituted, or it may be used as an alternative response between the verses:

Rest eternal grant unto them, O Lord, and let light perpetual shine upon them.

CONVERSION OF ST PAUL • APOSTLES EVANGELISTS
Morning

36   *The City of God*   Isa 26.1–4, 7–9, 12

R   **Open the gates, and let the righteous enter.**

We have a strong city : with walls and ramparts built for our safety.

Open the gates! Let a righteous nation enter : a nation that keeps faith.   *R*

Lord, you keep those of firm purpose untroubled : because of their trust in you.

Trust in the Lord for ever : for he is an eternal rock.   *R*

The path of the righteous is smooth : and you, Lord, make level the way for the upright.

We have had regard to the path prescribed in your laws : your name and your renown are our heart's desire.   *R*

With all my heart I long for you in the night : at dawn I seek for you.

For when your laws prevail on earth : the inhabitants of the world learn what justice is.   *R*

Lord, you will bestow prosperity upon us : for in truth all our works are your doing.   *R*

REB

TEACHERS
Morning

37   *The Wisdom of the Lord*   Prov 9.1–6, 10, 12

R   **The fear of the Lord is the beginning of wisdom.**

Wisdom has built her house, she has hewn her seven pillars : now having slaughtered a beast, spiced her wine and spread her table,

She has sent her maidens to proclaim from the highest point of the town : Let the simple turn in here.   *R*

She says to him who lacks sense : Come and eat the food I
have prepared and taste the wine that I have spiced.

Abandon the company of simpletons and you will live : you
will advance in understanding.   *R*

The first step to wisdom is the fear of the Lord : and
knowledge of the Most Holy One is understanding.

If you are wise, it will be to your advantage : if you are
arrogant, you alone must bear the blame.   *R*

REB

ABBOTS AND ABBESSES
Morning

38   *A Holy People*   Wisd 10.15–19, 20b–21

R   **Let us sing the glories of your name, O Lord.**

It was wisdom who rescued a godfearing people : a blameless
race from a nation of oppressors.

She inspired a servant of the Lord : and with his signs and
wonders he defied formidable kings.   *R*

She rewarded the labours of a godfearing people : she guided
them on a miraculous journey

And became a covering for them by day : and a blaze of stars
by night.   *R*

She brought them over the Red Sea : leading them through
its deep waters.

But their enemies she engulfed : and cast them up again out
of the fathomless deep.   *R*

Your people sang the glories of your name, O Lord : and
with one accord praised your power, their champion.

For wisdom enabled the dumb to speak : and made the
tongues of infants eloquent.   *R*

REB

MISSIONARIES
Morning

39   ***The Lord, the Redeemer***   Isa 49.8–13

R   **The one who loves them will lead them by springs of water.**

In the time of my favour I answered you : on the day of
deliverance I came to your aid.

I have formed you, and destined you to be a light to the
peoples : restoring the land and allotting once more its
desolate holdings.   *R*

I said to the prisoners, Go free : and to those in darkness,
Come out into the open.

Along every path they will find pasture : and grazing in all
the arid places.   *R*

They will neither hunger nor thirst : nor will scorching heat
or sun distress them.

For one who loves them will guide them : and lead them by
springs of water.   *R*

I shall make every hill a path : and raise up my highways.

They are coming, some from far away : some from the north
and the west, and others from the land of Syene.   *R*

Shout for joy, you heavens, earth rejoice : break into songs
of triumph, you mountains.

For the Lord has comforted his people : and has had pity on
their distress.   *R*

REB

MYSTICS

Morning

40   *The Works of the Lord*   *Ecclus 39.13, 22, 14–16a*

R   **Give thanks to him with praise and singing of songs.**

Listen to me, my devout sons : and blossom like a rose planted by a stream.

His blessing is like a river in full flood : which soaks the parched ground.   *R*

Spread your fragrance like frankincense : and bloom like a lily.

Scatter your fragrance, lift your voices in song : praising the Lord for all he has done.   *R*

Ascribe majesty to his name and give thanks to him : with praise, with harps and singing of songs.

Let these be your words of thanksgiving : all that the Lord has done is excellent.   *R*

REB

WOMEN SAINTS (Alternative A)
Morning

41   *Sing to My Lord*   *Judith 16.2–3, 13–16*

R   **O Lord, you are great and glorious, marvellous in your strength.**

Sing to the Lord with cymbals : strike up a song to my God with tambourines.

Raise a psalm of praise to him, honour him and invoke his name : the Lord is a God who stamps out wars.   *R*

I will sing a new hymn to my God : O Lord, you are great and glorious.

You are marvellous in your strength : invincible.   *R*

Let your whole creation serve you : for you spoke and all things came to be.

You sent out your spirit and it gave them form : none can oppose your word.   *R*

Mountains will shake to their depths like water, rocks melt like wax at your presence : but you still show compassion to those who fear you.

All sacrifices with their fragrance are but a small thing : but he who fears the Lord is great always.   *R*

REB

WOMEN SAINTS (Alternative B)
Morning or Evening

42   *A Song of God's Love*   *(based on Anselm)*

R   **(choice from lines marked *)**

*   Jesus, as a mother you gather your people to you :
you are gentle with us as a mother with her children.

Often you weep over our sins and our pride : tenderly you draw us from hatred and judgement.   *R*

You comfort us in sorrow and bind up our wounds : in sickness you nurse us, and with pure milk you feed us.

*   Jesus, by your dying we are born to new life :

*   by your anguish and labour we come forth in joy.   *R*

*   Despair turns to hope through your sweet goodness :
through your gentleness we find comfort in fear.

Your warmth gives life to the dead : your touch makes
sinners righteous.   *R*

Lord Jesus, in your mercy heal us : in your love and
tenderness remake us.

In your compassion bring grace and forgiveness : for the
beauty of heaven may your love prepare us.   *R*

Michael Vasey, In Penitence and Faith
(Music for this canticle may be obtained from Westcott House, Cambridge)

EMBERTIDE
Morning
43   *The Ministers of the Lord*   *Isa 61.6–9*

R   **Everlasting joy will be ours, a race blessed by the Lord.**

You will be called priests of the Lord : and be named
ministers of our God.

You will enjoy the wealth of nations : and succeed to
their riches.   *R*

And so, because shame in double measure : and insults and
abuse have been my people's lot,

They will receive in their own land a double measure of
wealth : and everlasting joy will be theirs.   *R*

For I, the Lord, love justice : and hate robbery and crime.

I shall grant them a sure reward : and make an everlasting
covenant with them.   *R*

Their posterity will be renowned among the nations : and
their descendants among the peoples.

All who see them will acknowledge : that they are a race
blessed by the Lord.   *R*

REB

CHRISTIAN UNITY
Morning

44   ***The Return to Zion***   *Ecclus 36.11–17*

R   **Listen, O Lord, to the prayer of your servants.**

Gather all the tribes of Jacob : and grant them their inheritance, as you did long ago.

Have pity, Lord, on the people called by your name : on Israel, whom you have named your firstborn.   *R*

Show mercy to the city of your sanctuary : to the city of Jerusalem, your dwelling place.

Fill Zion with the praise of your triumph : and the temple with your glory.   *R*

Acknowledge those you created at the beginning : and fulfil the prophecies spoken in your name.

Reward those who look to you in trust : prove your prophets worthy of credence.   *R*

Listen, O Lord, to the prayer of your servants : who claim Aaron's blessing on your people.

Let all who live on earth acknowledge : that you are the Lord, the eternal God.   *R*

REB

DEDICATION FESTIVAL
CONSECRATION OF A CHURCH
Morning

45   ***The Temple of the Lord***   *Jer 7.2–7*

R   **Let us stand at the gate of the Lord's house and proclaim his word.**

Hear the word of the Lord, all you of Judah : who come in through these gates to worship him.

These are the words of the Lord of Hosts, the God of Israel : Amend your ways and your deeds, that I may let you live in this place.   *R*

You keep saying, This place is the temple of the Lord : the temple of the Lord, the temple of the Lord!

If you amend your ways and your deeds, deal fairly with one another : cease to oppress the alien, the fatherless, and the widow, *R*

If you shed no innocent blood in this place : and do not run after other gods to your own ruin,

Then I shall let you live in this place : in the land which long ago I gave to your forefathers for all time. *R*

REB

SUNDAYS (except Seventh before Christmas to Advent 4 and Epiphany 1)
THANKSGIVING FOR HOLY COMMUNION
Evening

46   *A Song of Faith and Hope*   *I Pet 1.3–4, 18–21*

R   **Praised be the God and Father of our Lord Jesus Christ.**

In his great mercy by the resurrection of Jesus Christ from the dead : he gave us new birth into a living hope,

The hope of an inheritance, reserved in heaven for you : which nothing can destroy or spoil or wither. *R*

It was nothing of passing value like silver or gold : that bought your freedom from the futility of your traditional ways.

You were set free by Christ's precious blood : blood like that of a lamb without mark or blemish. *R*

He was predestined before the foundation of the world : but in this last period of time he has been revealed for your sake.

Through him you have come to trust in God who raised him from the dead and gave him glory : and so your faith and hope are fixed on God. *R*

REB

MONDAY • BLESSED VIRGIN MARY
(CONCEPTION**)
NATIVITY (FALLING ASLEEP**)
BAPTISM • CONFIRMATION
Evening

47 *A Song of God's Grace* *Eph 1.3–10*

R* **God has made known to us his secret purpose in Christ.**

Blessed be the God and Father of our Lord Jesus Christ : who has conferred on us in Christ every spiritual blessing in the heavenly realms.

Before the foundation of the world he chose us in Christ to be his people : to be without blemish in his sight. *R*

And he predestined us to be adopted : as his children through Jesus Christ.

This was his will and pleasure : in order that the glory of his gracious gift so graciously conferred on us in the Beloved might redound to his praise. *R*

In Christ our release is secured : and our sins forgiven through the shedding of his blood.

In the richness of his grace : God has lavished on us all wisdom and insight. *R*

He has made known to us his secret purpose : in accordance with the plan which he determined beforehand in Christ

To be put into effect when the time was ripe : namely that the universe, everything in heaven and on earth, might be brought into a unity in Christ. *R*

REB

*Alternative for (1) BAPTISM and CONFIRMATION, and (2) BVM:

(1)*R* **He has conferred on us every spiritual blessing.**
(2)*R* **Before the foundation of the world, Mary was chosen.**

***See notes on Canticle 33*

TUESDAY • HOLY CROSS DAY
DEDICATION OR CONSECRATION OF A
CHURCH

Evening

48   *Glory and Honour*   *Rev 4.9–11; 5.9–10, 13*

R   **Glory and honour are yours for ever, Lord God.**

Glory and honour and power :
    are yours by right O Lord our God:

for you created all things :
    and by your will they have their being.   *R*

Glory and honour and power :
    are yours by right O Lamb who was slain;

for by your blood you ransomed men for God :
    from every race and language, from every people and
        nation,   *R*

to make them a kingdom of priests :
    to stand and serve before our God.

To him who sits on the throne and to the Lamb :
    be praise and honour, glory and might for ever and ever.
        Amen.   *R*

ASB

WEDNESDAY • PRESENTATION OF CHRIST
DEDICATION OR CONSECRATION OF A CHURCH
Evening

49   *Christ the Firstborn*   Col 1.12–20

R* **In Christ the firstborn, God will reconcile all things to himself.**

Let us give joyful thanks to the Father : who has made us fit to share the heritage of God's people in the realm of light.

He rescued us from the domain of darkness, and brought us into the kingdom of his dear Son : through whom our release is secured and our sins are forgiven.   *R*

He is the image of the invisible God : his is the primacy over all creation.

In him everything in heaven and on earth was created : not only things visible   *R*

But also the invisible orders of thrones : sovereignties, authorities and powers.

The whole universe has been created : through him and for him.   *R*

He exists before all things : and all things are held together in him.

He is the head of the body, the Church, he is its origin : the first to return from the dead to become in all things supreme.   *R*

For in him, God in all his fullness chose to dwell : and through him to reconcile all things to himself,

Making peace through the shedding of his blood on the cross : all things whether on earth or in heaven.   *R*

REB

*Alternative for (1) PRESENTATION, and (2) CONSECRATION/DEDICATION:
(1)*R* **He has rescued us from the dominion of darkness.**
(2)*R* **He is the head of the body, the Church.**

THURSDAY • MAUNDY THURSDAY
CHRISTIAN UNITY
Evening

50   *A Song of Love*   *I John 4. 7–8; I Cor 13.4–10, 12, 13*

*R** **Let us love one another, for love is of God.**

Let us love one another : because the source of love is God.

Everyone who loves is a child of God and knows God : but the unloving know nothing of God, for God is love.   *R*

Love is patient and kind, love envies no one : love is never boastful, never conceited, never rude.

Love is never selfish, never quick to take offence : love keeps no score of wrongs.   *R*

Love takes no pleasure in the sins of others : but delights in the truth.

There is nothing love cannot face : there is no limit to its faith, its hope, its endurance.   *R*

Love will never come to an end, prophecies will cease : tongues of ecstasy will fall silent, knowledge will vanish,

For our knowledge and our prophecy alike are partial : and the partial vanishes when wholeness comes.   *R*

My knowledge now is partial : then it will be whole like God's knowledge of me.

There are three things that last for ever, faith, hope, and love : and the greatest of the three is love.   *R*

REB

*Alternative for UNITY:

R **Love keeps no score of wrongs, but delights in the truth.**

FRIDAY • SOCIAL RESPONSIBILITY
Evening

51 *Great and Wonderful*   Rev 15.3–4; 5.13

R*   **Great and wonderful is the Lord God almighty.**

Great and wonderful are your deeds, Lord God the
Almighty :
    just and true are your ways, O King of the nations.

Who shall not revere and praise your name, O Lord? :
    for you alone are holy.   *R*

All nations shall come and worship in your presence :
    for your just dealings have been revealed.

To him who sits on the throne and to the Lamb :
    be praise and honour, glory and might
    for ever and ever. Amen.   *R*

ASB

*Alternative for SOCIAL RESPONSIBILITY:
R   **Just and true are the ways of the righteous God.**

SATURDAY • NAMING OF JESUS to day
before Epiphany • ASCENSION • HOLY
CROSS DAY
Evening

52 *A Song of Christ's Glory*   Phil 2.5–11

R*   **Let every tongue confess that Christ is Lord.**

Christ Jesus was in the form of God :
    but he did not cling to equality with God.

He emptied himself, taking the form of a servant :
    and was born in the likeness of men.   *R*

Being found in human form he humbled himself :
    and became obedient unto death even death on a cross.

Therefore God has highly exalted him :
    and bestowed on him the name above every name,   *R*

that at the name of Jesus every knee should bow :
    in heaven and on earth and under the earth;

and every tongue confess that Jesus Christ is Lord :
   to the glory of God the Father.   *R*

ASB

*Alternatives for (1) NAMING OF JESUS, (2) HOLY CROSS,
(3) ASCENSION:
(1)*R* **At the name of Jesus every knee should bow.**
(2)*R* **He became obedient to death on a cross.**
(3)*R* **God has highly exalted him, Alleluia!**

BEFORE ADVENT
SUNDAYS (Third before Advent to Advent 4)
CHRIST THE KING
Evening

53   *A Song of the Lamb*   *Rev 19.1b, 2, 5, 6b, 7, 9; 5.13*

R   **Alleluia.**

Victory and glory and power belong to our God : for true
and just are his judgements!   *R*

Praise our God, all you his servants : you that fear him, both
small and great!   *R*

The Lord our God, sovereign over all : has entered on
his reign!   *R*

Let us rejoice and shout for joy and pay homage to him : for
the wedding day of the Lamb has come.   *R*

His bride has made herself ready : happy are those who are
invited to the wedding banquet of the Lamb!   *R*

**To him who sits on the throne and to the Lamb : be praise
and honour, glory and might, for ever and ever, Amen.**   *R*

REB

(Doxology ASB)

BEFORE ADVENT
WEEKDAYS (Monday after Third before Advent
to day before Advent 1)
Evening

54 ***A Song of the Spirit*** *Rev 22.12–14, 16b, 17, 20*

R   Surely, I am coming soon. Amen, come, Lord Jesus.

I am coming soon, and bringing with me my recompense : to repay everyone according to what he has done.

I am the Alpha and the Omega, the first and the last : the beginning and the end.   *R*

Happy are those who wash their robes clean : they shall be free to eat from the tree of life, and may enter the city by the gates.

I am the offspring of David, the shoot growing from his stock : the bright star of dawn.   *R*

Come, say the Spirit and the Bride : Come, let each hearer reply.

Let the thirsty come : let whoever wishes accept the water of life as a gift.   *R*

REB

ADVENT

WEEKDAYS (day after Advent 1 to December 16)
Evening

55 ***Advent Prose***   *Isa 40.1; 43.10, 13, 14; 44.22; 45.8; 64.6, 7, 8, 10*

R **Pour down, O heavens, from above : and let the skies rain down righteousness.**

Turn your fierce anger from us, O Lord : and remember not our sins for ever.

Your holy cities have become a desert – Zion a desert : Jerusalem a desolation; our holy and beautiful house, where our fathers praised you.   *R*

We have sinned and become like one who is unclean : we have all withered like a leaf, and our iniquities, like the wind, have swept us away.

You have hidden your face from us : and abandoned us to our iniquities.   *R*

You are my witnesses, says the Lord; and my servant whom I have chosen : that you may know me and believe me.

I myself am the Lord, and none but I can deliver : what my hand holds none can snatch away.   *R*

Comfort my people, comfort them : my salvation shall not be delayed.

I have swept your offences away like a cloud : fear not, for I will save you.

I am the Lord your God : the Holy one of Israel, your redeemer.   *R*

Brother Reginald SSF

(Doxology normally omitted)

This arrangement has been made to go with the plainsong melody in the *Liber Usualis* and the *English Hymnal*.

ADVENT

WEEKDAYS (December 17 to 24)

Evening

56 *Advent Antiphons*

R **(Please note that this changes for each verse)**

O Wisdom, you come forth from the mouth of the Most
High : you fill the universe and hold all things together with
gentle strength.

R **Come, Lord Jesus : come and teach us the way of truth!**

O Adonai and Leader of Israel, you appeared to Moses in a
burning bush : and gave him the law on Sinai.

R **Come, Lord Jesus : come and set us free with your mighty
power!**

O Stock of Jesse, you stand as an ensign for the nations :
kings fall silent before you whom the nations long for.

R **Come, Lord Jesus : come and deliver us without delay!**

O Key of David and Sceptre of Israel, what you open no one
can close : and what you close no one can open.

R **Come, Lord Jesus, come and deliver the captive from prison :
free those who sit in darkness and in the shadow of death!**

O Rising Sun, you are the splendour of eternal light : and the
sun of righteousness.

R **Come, Lord Jesus, come and enlighten those who sit in
darkness : and in the shadow of death!**

O King of the nations and their desire : you are the
cornerstone which makes both one.

R **Come, Lord Jesus : come and save man whom you formed
from clay!**

O Emmanuel, you are our King and our Judge : the one for
whom the nations yearn, and their Saviour.

R **Come, Lord Jesus : come and save, our Lord and God.**

(Doxology normally omitted)

(This version from *Prayers for Alternative Services* by D. Silk,
arranged for responsorial recitation by the compiler.)

57   *A Song of the Incarnation*   Mal 4.2; Isa 9.2, 6a; I John 4.9;
II Cor 8.9; Heb 1.2; John 1.14

R   **The Word was made flesh and dwelt among us.**

The grace of God has dawned upon the world : with healing
for all mankind.

The people who walked in darkness have seen a great light :
light has dawned upon us, dwellers in a land as dark
as death.   *R*

For a boy has been born to us : a son given us.

God is love, and his love was disclosed to us in this : that he
sent his only Son into the world to bring us life.   *R*

We know how generous our Lord Jesus Christ has been : he
was rich, yet for our sake he became poor, so that through
his poverty we might become rich.

God has spoken to us in his Son : whom he has made heir to
the whole universe.   *R*

The Word became flesh : he came to dwell among us.

And we saw his glory : such glory as befits the Father's only
Son, full of grace and truth.   *R*

Hymns and Psalms

EPIPHANY to EPIPHANY 1 • ASCENSION
TRANSFIGURATION • MICHAELMAS
CHRIST THE KING
Evening

58   *The Song of Glory Revealed*   *I Tim 3.16; 6.15, 16*

R   **Alleluia.**

Christ was manifested in flesh : he was vindicated in
spirit.   **R**

Christ was seen by angels : he was proclaimed among
the nations.   **R**

Christ was believed in throughout the world : he was raised
to heavenly glory.   **R**

He is the blessed and only Sovereign : King of kings and Lord
of lords.   **R**

He alone possesses immortality : dwelling in
unapproachable light.   **R**

Him no one has seen or can ever see : to him be honour and
dominion for ever! Amen.   **R**

REB

SUNDAYS IN LENT
ASH WEDNESDAY to day before Lent 1
Evening

59   *A Song of Saint John*   *I John 1.5–9*

R   **The blood of Jesus cleanses us from all sin.**

God is light :
    and in him is no darkness at all.

If we say we have fellowship with him while we walk in
    darkness :
    we lie and do not live according to the truth.   **R**

But if we walk in the light as he is in the light :
    we have fellowship with one another.

And the blood of Jesus his Son :
    cleanses us from all sin.   **R**

If we say we have no sin :
   we deceive ourselves and the truth is not in us.

If we confess our sins :
   he is faithful and just.   *R*

He will forgive our sins :
   and will cleanse us from all unrighteousness.   *R*

In Penitence and Faith

LENT (day after Lent 1 to day before Lent 3)
Evening

60   ***A Song of Assurance***   *Rom 8.28, 29a, 30, 31b, 32–35, 36b, 37*

R   **Who can separate us from the love of Christ?**

In everything God co-operates for good : with those who love him and are called according to his purpose,

For those whom God knew before ever they were : he also ordained to share the likeness of his Son,   *R*

And those whom he foreordained he also called : and those whom he called he also justified,

And those whom he justified : he also glorified.   *R*

If God is on our side : who is against us?

He did not spare his own Son, but gave him up for us all : how can he fail to lavish every other gift upon us?   *R*

Who will bring a charge against those whom God has chosen? : not God who acquits.

Who will pronounce judgement? : not Christ who died, or rather rose again.   *R*

Not Christ who is at God's right hand : and pleads our cause.

Then what can separate us from the love of Christ : can affliction or hardship?   *R*

Can persecution, hunger, nakedness : danger, or sword?

We have been treated like sheep for slaughter : and yet overwhelming victory is ours through him who loved us.   *R*

REB

LENT

WEEKDAYS (day after Lent 3 to day before Lent 5)
Evening

61 *Saviour of the World*

R **Lord Jesus, you are our mighty deliverer.**

Jesus, Saviour of the world,
  come to us in your mercy :
we look to you to save and help us.

By your cross and your life laid down,
  you set your people free :
we look to you to save and help us. *R*

When they were ready to perish,
  you saved your disciples :
we look to you to come to our help.

In the greatness of your mercy,
  loose us from our chains :
forgive the sins of all your people. *R*

Make yourself known as our saviour and
  mighty deliverer :
save and help us that we may praise you.

Come now and dwell with us, Lord Christ Jesus :
hear our prayer and be with us always. *R*

And when you come in your glory :
make us to be one with you
  and to share the life of your kingdom. *R*

ASB

LENT
WEEKDAYS (day after Lent 5 to Wednesday in Holy Week)
HOLY CROSS DAY • EMBERTIDE
Evening

62   *A Song of Christ the Servant*   *1 Pet 2.21–25*

R   (LENT, HOLY CROSS) **Christ bore our sins in his body on the tree.**

R   (EMBERTIDE) **We have the example of Christ, the guardian of our souls.**

Christ himself suffered on your behalf, and left you an example : in order that you should follow in his steps.

He committed no sin, he was guilty of no falsehood : when he was abused he did not retaliate.   *R*

When he suffered he uttered no threats : but delivered himself up to him who judges justly.

He carried our sins in his own person on the gibbet : so that we might cease to live for sin and begin to live for righteousness.   *R*

By his wounds : you have been healed.

You were straying like sheep : but now you have turned towards the Shepherd and Guardian of your souls.   *R*

REB

MAUNDY THURSDAY (if the Maundy Thursday
Liturgy is not celebrated)
CHRISTIAN UNITY
Evening

63 *Ubi Caritas*

R **God is love, and where true love is, God himself is there.**

Here in Christ, we gather, love of Christ our calling;
Christ, our love, is with us, gladness be his greeting;
Let us all revere and love him, God eternal :
Loving him, let each love Christ in all his brothers. **R**

When we Christians gather, members of one Body,
Let there be in us no discord, but one spirit;
Banished now be anger, strife and every quarrel :
Christ our God be present always here among us. **R**

Grant us love's fulfilment, joy with all the blessed,
When we see your face, O Saviour, in its glory;
Shine on us, O purest Light of all creation,
Be our bliss while endless ages sing your praises. **R**

James Quinn

(If sung, the tune is found in NEH 513. Other versions of this canticle can be
used.)

GOOD FRIDAY (if the Good Friday Liturgy is not
celebrated)
Evening

64 *Anthem 1*

R (*see verse so marked below*)

We glory in your cross, O Lord :
and praise you for your mighty resurrection;

R **For by virtue of your cross :**
joy has come into the world.

God be gracious and bless us :
and make his face shine upon us.

Let your ways be known on earth :
your liberating power among all nations.   *R*

Let the people praise you, O God :
let all the peoples praise you.

We glory in your cross, O Lord :
and praise you for your mighty resurrection;

R   **For by virtue of your cross :
joy has come into our world.**

Lent, Holy Week and Easter

(Doxology omitted)

(As an alternative any other anthem for Good Friday from *Lent,
Holy Week and Easter* may be used)

EASTER EVE (if the Easter Liturgy is not celebrated at night)

Evening

65   *A Song of Salvation*   *Rom 5.1–3, 5, 6, 8; 8.37*

R   **Overwhelming victory is ours through him who loved us.**

Now that we have been justified through faith : we are at
peace with God through our Lord Jesus Christ

Who has given us access to that grace in which we now live :
and we exult in the hope of the divine glory that is to be
ours.   *R*

More than this, we even exult in our present sufferings :
because we know that suffering is a source of endurance.

Such hope is no fantasy : through the Holy Spirit he has
given us, God's love has flooded our hearts.   *R*

It was while we were still helpless : that, at the appointed
time, Christ died for the wicked.

Christ died for us while we were yet sinners : and that is
God's proof of his love towards us.   *R*

REB

EASTERTIDE (Easter 1 to day before Ascension)
BAPTISM • CONFIRMATION
Evening

66   *The River of Life*   *Ezek 47.1b; Rev 22.1, 2; 21.6b*

R*   **Alleluia.**

I saw a spring of water issuing towards the east : from under
the threshold of the temple.   *R*

The water was running down along the south side : to the
right of the altar.   *R*

The angel showed me the river of the water of life : sparkling
like crystal,   *R*

Flowing from the throne of God and of the Lamb : down the
middle of the city's street.   *R*

On either side of the river stood a tree of life : which yields
twelve crops of fruit, one for each month of the year.   *R*

The leaves of the trees : are for the healing of the nations.   *R*

To the thirsty I will give water : from the spring of life as
a gift.   *R*

REB

*Alternative for BAPTISM and CONFIRMATION:

R   **To the thirsty I will give the water of life.**

EASTERTIDE (Easter 1 to day before Ascension)
BAPTISM • CONFIRMATION
Evening

67 *Easter Sequence*

R **Christians, to the Paschal Victim offer sacrifice and praise.**

The sheep are ransomed by the Lamb, and Christ the
    undefiled :
  has sinners to his Father reconciled.

Death with life contended :
  combat strangely ended.   *R*

Life's own champion, slain :
  yet lives to reign.

Tell us, Mary, say :
  what did you see upon the way?   *R*

The tomb the living did enclose:
  I saw Christ's glory as he rose.

The angels there attesting:
  shroud with grave-clothes resting.   *R*

Christ, my hope, has risen:
  he goes before you into Galilee.

That Christ is truly risen from the dead we know :
  Victorious King, your mercy show!   *R*

Roman Missal

(A plainchant setting of this canticle in traditional language can be
found in *New English Hymnal*, no. 519)

ASCENSION to PENTECOST
GUIDANCE OF THE HOLY SPIRIT
BAPTISM • CONFIRMATION
Evening

68   *The Promise of the Coming Spirit*   *Joel 2.28; John 14.16, 26; Rom 8.26*

R*   **The Spirit intercedes for us with sighs too deep for words.**

I shall pour out my spirit on all mankind : your sons and daughters will prophesy.

Your old men will dream dreams : and your young men see visions.   *R*

I will ask the Father and he will give you another to be your advocate : who will be with you for ever, the Spirit of truth.

The advocate, the Holy Spirit whom the Father will send in my name : will teach you everything and remind you of all that I have told you.   *R*

In the same way the Spirit comes to the aid of our weakness : we do not even know how we ought to pray.

But through our inarticulate groans : the Spirit himself is pleading for us.   *R*

REB

*Alternative for BAPTISM and CONFIRMATION:
R   **The Holy Spirit will lead us in the way of truth.**

VISIT OF MARY TO ELIZABETH
MARY MAGDALEN • MYSTICS • WOMEN
SAINTS
Evening

69   *Christ the Mother*   *(based on Julian of Norwich)*

R   **A mother's care is kindest, for it is most true.**

A mother's care is kindest, for it is most true :
this care cannot be done in full except by
    Christ himself.   *R*

Our own mother bore us into pain and dying :
Our true mother, Jesus, bears us into endless living.

A mother feeds her child with her milk :
Our mother, Jesus, feeds us with his blessed self.   *R*

A mother may allow her child to be unhappy :
Jesus may let us sorrow, yet he weeps with us for love.

As a child grows, a mother allows it to be punished :
Our Lord does the same thing as we grow in strength.   *R*

An earthly mother may allow her child to die :
Our heavenly mother, Jesus, will not let his children
    perish.

A mother's care is kindest, for it is most true :
this care cannot be done in full except by
    Christ himself.   *R*

Sheila Upjohn

70   *A Song of the Redeemed*   Rev 7.9–10, 14b–17

R*   **Salvation belongs to our God who sits on the throne.**

I looked and saw a vast throng which no one could count :
from all races and tribes, nations and languages, standing
before the throne and the Lamb.

They were robed in white : and had palm branches in
their hands.   *R*

And they shouted aloud : Victory to our God who sits on the
throne, and to the Lamb.

They are those who have passed through the great ordeal :
they have washed their robes and made them white in the
blood of the Lamb.   *R*

That is why they stand before the throne of God : and
worship him day and night in his temple.

And he who sits on the throne : will protect them with
his presence.   *R*

Never again shall they feel hunger or thirst : never again shall
the sun beat on them or any scorching heat,

Because the Lamb who is at the centre of the throne will be
their shepherd : and will guide them to springs of the water
of life.   *R*

REB

*Alternative for MARTYRS and JOHN THE BAPTIST:

R   **The white-robed army of martyrs praise you.**

71 *A Song of the Holy City*   Rev 21.1–5a

R*   **Rest eternal grant unto them, O Lord, and let light perpetual shine upon them.**

I saw a new heaven and a new earth, for the first heaven and the first earth had vanished : and there was no longer any sea.

I saw the Holy City, new Jerusalem, coming down out of heaven from God : made ready like a bride adorned for her husband.   *R*

I heard a loud voice proclaiming from the throne : now God has his dwelling with mankind.

He will dwell among them, and they shall be his people : and God himself will be with them.   *R*

He will wipe away every tear from their eyes, there shall be an end to death : and to mourning and crying and pain, for the old order has passed away.

The One who sat on the throne said : I am making all things new.   *R*

REB

*Alternative:

R   **There shall be an end to death, and God shall be with them.**

TIMOTHY AND TITUS • TEACHERS
BISHOPS • ABBOTS AND ABBESSES
MISSIONARIES • ANY SAINT
Evening

72 *A Song of God's Judgement*   Rev 11.17–18; 12.10–12a

R   Now is the time for rewarding the prophets and saints.

O Lord God, sovereign over all : you are and you were.

We give you thanks because you have assumed full power :
and entered upon your reign.   **R**

The nations rose in wrath, but your day of wrath has come :
now is the time for the dead to be judged.

Now is the time for rewards to be given to your servants the
prophets, to your own people : and to all who honour your
name, both small and great.   **R**

This is the time of victory for our God, the time of his power
and sovereignty : when his Christ comes to his rightful rule.

For the accuser of our brothers : he who day and night
accused them before our God is overthrown.   **R**

By the sacrifice of the Lamb and by the witness they bore :
they have conquered him; faced with death, they did not
cling to life.

Therefore, rejoice you heavens : and you that dwell
in them.   **R**

REB

The Intercessions

SUNDAY (except BEFORE ADVENT, ADVENT, LENT)

1a Morning

Father, we praise you on this first day of the new creation :
with joy we come to greet the risen Lord.

R **This is the day of the Lord; let us be glad.**

Father, you are without beginning or end : give us a glimpse
of eternity and a deeper desire for you in the
eucharist today. **R**

Father, your ways are unknowable, hidden in the realms of
inaccessible light : may we know your Son in the breaking of
the bread. **R**

Father, none can equal you in power and might : in your
invincible strength alone shall we overcome the enemy and
rise victorious over death. **R**

Let us join the prophets, apostles and martyrs and all the
angels and saints in the hymn of your
everlasting praise. **R**

Compiler

1b Evening

The prophets foretold the Messiah's banquet in which all nations would share : Lord, we rejoice that your name is hailed in all the world today.

R **Lord, hasten your kingdom.**

Lord, you fed the multitude when they were hungry and told them to seek the bread of eternal life : we give thanks for the most holy eucharist. *R*

Man does not live by bread alone, but by every word of yours : we give thanks that we have fed today upon your most holy word. *R*

Not all who were called entered the wedding feast, and the disadvantaged took their places : strengthen us to go out and show your love to the needy. *R*

We are all baptized into the death and resurrection of your Son : may we, and all who have gone before us in the faith, be clothed in immortality and enter the marriage feast of the Lamb. *R*

When the disciples were afraid and the doors were closed you came and greeted them in your peace : send us out boldly in the peace and power of the Spirit. *R*

Compiler

MONDAY

2a Morning

Lord, you have sanctified the labour of our hands by your incarnation : fashion us with the tools of our salvation as we pray that our work this week may proclaim your purpose.

R **May all we begin, be continued and ended in you.**

Lord, you toiled at the carpenter's trade : we pray for all who work in industry and commerce, in agriculture and at sea. *R*

Lord, you offered to the heavily laden your easy yoke : we pray for all whose labour is hard, monotonous or exposes them to danger. *R*

Lord, your ministry took you far from home : we pray for all who serve their country abroad, and those whose work parts them from their families. *R*

Lord, you constantly met the demands of the needy : we pray for all whose work is deeply demanding or causes them stress. *R*

Compiler

2b Evening

Let us give thanks for all that we have begun in your name today : Father, through the sacrifice of your Son, complete and perfect our small beginnings.

R **May all things be done in the Name of the Lord Jesus.**

Give us a true concern for the unemployed : we pray for all who lack a sense of belonging. *R*

Give courage to the disabled : and may we grow to understand their needs. *R*

Reward with a sense of achievement all who are unable to sustain work : we pray for those who help them. *R*

Bring healing to all who suffer industrial disease : and may we continue to work for its prevention. *R*

Give us a deeper concern for safety at work and for proper conditions : we remember those who today have died in the course of their work. *R*

Compiler

TUESDAY

3a Morning

Most holy Trinity, we praise and thank you for your creative
and redemptive power and for life in the Spirit.

R **May the Holy Spirit rule in our hearts.**

You made us in your image and likeness : enable us to use
our skills for your glory and the service of others. ***R***

We thank you for the joy and wisdom we gain from art,
music, literature and drama : we pray for all whose gifts in
these things give us pleasure. ***R***

We give thanks for the beauty of the world around us : we
pray for all who are caring for the environment and shaping
it for the future. ***R***

Lord, we have brought waste, ugliness and alienation into a
world you made perfect : deepen our respect for life and the
systems you created to support it. ***R***

Compiler

3b Evening

We pray for all who work in the media and publishing : may
their quest be for truth and honesty.

R **Lord, keep us true to our calling.**

We pray for all in the caring and healing professions : may
their task be fulfilled in love. ***R***

We pray for those called to government, politics and law :
may their search be for security, justice and right. ***R***

We pray for all who teach and carry out research : may their
love be for learning. ***R***

We pray for all who defend their country in armed service :
may their desire be for peace. ***R***

We give thanks for all the essential services that others
provide for us : and for their readiness to serve at all
times. ***R***

Compiler

WEDNESDAY

4a Morning

Lord Jesus Christ, you called your disciples to follow in your steps : may we follow you more closely day by day.

R **Lord, make us attentive to your call.**

Let us pray that all Christians may discern the nature of their calling as we serve Christ in the world. *R*

Let us give thanks for all who have answered the call to the ordained ministry. *R*

Let us give thanks for all who have found their vocation in the religious life. *R*

Let us pray for all whose vocation is being tested at this time, and those who are assisting them. *R*

Let us pray for the young and those who teach them, as they seek to determine their calling in life. *R*

Compiler

4b Evening

Merciful Lord, Joseph and Mary knew the anxiety of losing your Son in the temple : we pray for all whose family life is in difficulty.

R **Loving Father, look upon your children.**

Let us pray for all who are striving to bring up their children in the way of Christ : may they act with gentleness in strength. *R*

Let us pray for the children of unhappy, broken and violent homes. *R*

Let us pray for parents who are unable to give each other and their children security and love. *R*

Let us pray for all who live alone and those who have no families : comfort them with your abiding presence. *R*

Let us pray for all who mourn the loss of a child, and for all in bereavement. *R*

Compiler

THURSDAY

5a Morning

Let us give thanks for the Bride of Christ, the Church : may the Spirit guide her into all truth.

R **Lord, cherish your Church.**

Let us pray for our archbishop N, and Nn, the bishop(s) of this diocese : may they be true pastors of their flock. *R*

Let us pray for the unity of Christ's Church in the time and manner that he wills, and for our fellow Christians in this place. *R*

Let us pray for this deanery and for this parish and all who minister here (especially Nn). *R*

Let us pray for the synods of the Church : may their members discern the mind of Christ. *R*

Compiler

5b Evening

Lord Jesus, at the Last Supper you gave the new commandment to love as you have loved us. May we live in unity and charity with our brothers and sisters.

R **May we love others as you love us.**

Let us give thanks for the feast of love and fellowship : we pray for the nourishment of our Christian lives. *R*

Where true love is found, God is dwelling there : banish the darkness from our hearts and discord from our lives. *R*

Let us give thanks for the eternal offering of Christ to the Father : may all our lives be an offering of love and sacrifice to one another and to God. *R*

Let us give thanks for the power of the love of Christ to heal and save, especially in the sacraments of the Church. *R*

We pray for those nearest and dearest to us : may our departed be upheld in the love of Christ. *R*

Compiler

FRIDAY

6a Morning

Holy God, holy and strong, as we reflect on the triumph of the cross we remember before you all who feel the sharpness of death today.

R **Holy and strong, have mercy upon us.**

To those on trial or under interrogation, grant your wise counsel and quiet eloquence. ***R***

To those broken by torture and persecution and to the mocked, bring the wholeness of your seamless robe. ***R***

To the imprisoned and the captive, grant the perfect freedom which is your service. ***R***

To the refugee, the exile and the homeless, make the promise of a lasting home in paradise. ***R***

To all under the threat of execution and sudden death, show your crown of thorns, the crown of glory. ***R***

Compiler

6b Evening

Most loving Lord, holy and immortal, by your cross and resurrection you have overcome the world. We pray tonight for all who lie in the shadow of the cross.

R   **Holy and immortal, have mercy upon us.**

Give healing to every broken life.   *R*

Give release to those consumed by bitterness.   *R*

Give light to those who sit in darkness.   *R*

Give peace to the tormented.   *R*

Give joy to those in despair.   *R*

Give relief to all in pain.   *R*

Give hope to the dying.   *R*

Give faith to the searching.   *R*

Compiler

SATURDAY

7a   Morning

Father, on the seventh day you rested from the work of creation and rejoiced in it: despite our unfaithfulness may we enter your rest.

R   **Grant us your rest.**

Father, we offer you all the achievements and failures of the past week : refresh us in mind and body and spirit to serve you once more.   **R**

Your Son enjoyed the company of a banquet, and provided wine for a wedding : may all our enjoyment of life be consecrated by him.   **R**

Your Son has left us the peace which the world cannot give : give us that peace in our hearts, our homes, and between nations today.   **R**

May rest be given to the weary and peace to the departed, so that they may rise again in glory.   **R**

Compiler

7b Evening

At the lighting of the evening lamps to greet the risen Lord we offer you our prayer and praise.

R **May we know you in the breaking of the bread.**

Lord, you spent nights in prayer with the Father : keep us alert to watch and pray with you. *R*

Lord, you were arrested and questioned in the hours of darkness : be present to all who are harassed by the powers of darkness. *R*

You spent a night in the tomb, but it could not contain you : free us from the prison of our sin as we prepare to receive you in our hearts. *R*

At the resurrection the new age dawned : as we look forward to your coming again, strengthen our hope in the sharing of the bread and the cup. *R*

Into your hands, Lord, we commend our spirit : may we rise in joy and go out to meet you in the eucharist. *R*

Compiler

BEFORE ADVENT
SUNDAYS AND WEEKDAYS
(Third Sunday before Advent to day before Advent 1)

8a Morning

God Almighty, we bless you for calling us to know you, to love and to serve you in spite of all we do wrong.

R **Maranatha, the Lord is coming!**

You have sent your beloved Son, your perfect image and the reflection of your glory : for our salvation you have revealed him in our humanity, intending him to be like us in all things but sin. *R*

In him you enlighten our ignorance by the light of the Gospel; you proclaim your Kingdom for us : you wash away our offences and you heal our infirmities. *R*

O God, you love all your creatures; keep us in the grace of Christ and the ways of his goodness : may we peacefully await the day when he returns in his glory. *R*

Grant us your peace; may we share it one with another in brotherly love and offer you our spiritual worship, consecrating our lives to your praise and to the service of our neighbours. *R*

Taizé

8b   Evening

God the Father, you desired neither sacrifices nor offerings, but you sent us your Beloved to reconcile all things in heaven and on earth through him, making peace by the blood of his cross.

R   **Glory to God who comes!**

God the Son, Saviour of the world, you have shared our humanity, you have been like us in all things but sin.   *R*

God the Holy Spirit, you descended on Christ in whom lives the fullness of godhead.   *R*

O Christ, may your incarnation and your birth make us love our human condition.   *R*

May your perfect knowledge of the Father's love strengthen us in the Way of Life.   *R*

May your faithfulness to your work make us each faithful in our vocation.   *R*

May your hidden life help us to live humbly.   *R*

Taizé

ADVENT (1 to December 16)
SUNDAYS AND WEEKDAYS

9a   Morning

Lord of the universe, all times are yours, and your purposes will surely be fulfilled. We eagerly await your coming in great power and glory.

R   **You are the beginning and end of all things.**

Lord, you have given us life and all that we have : prepare us for death by making us ever willing to surrender everything to you.   **R**

Lord, we believe that you will come to judge the living and the dead : we pray that you will look upon us then with pity, not with blame.   **R**

Lord, all that you have created is good, yet we have often preferred to disfigure and distort : save us from the pains of hell.   **R**

Lord, you created us, your children, to worship you and to inherit eternal life : kindle in our hearts a longing for the home you have promised us in heaven.   **R**

Compiler

9b **Evening**

John the Baptist was sent to prepare the way of the Lord, and preach a gospel of repentance. Prepare our hearts, Lord, to receive you whenever that time shall be.

R **Let us prepare a highway for our God.**

Lord, you were anointed by the Spirit to preach the Good News to the poor : may we learn true poverty of spirit and enter into their joy. *R*

Lord, you were anointed by the Spirit to release captives and victims of oppression : give hope to all who cry out in their suffering. *R*

The deaf hear, the blind see and the dumb speak, all declaring your wonderful works : let us proclaim and acknowledge the advent of the new order. *R*

Lord, in your kingdom all nations will be drawn to the Messiah's banquet where they will taste and be filled : from your goodness, supply the wants of all in need. *R*

Lord, in your kingdom justice and peace shall endure, and wickedness will be at an end : hasten your rule in all the world, that the nations may live at peace with one another and with you. *R*

Compiler

ADVENT (December 17–24)
SUNDAYS AND WEEKDAYS

10a Morning

Let the heavens open and the skies rain down the Just One :
let the earth bring forth Christ, who is the wisdom and
power of God.

R **Come, Lord Jesus, do not delay.**

Lord Jesus Christ, you have called us into your kingdom :
may we enter in and live according to your call. *R*

The world does not know you : show yourself in our midst
to all our brothers and sisters. *R*

We thank you, Lord, for all that we have : move us to give
of our plenty to those who have little. *R*

We look for your coming, Lord Jesus : when you knock may
we be found rejoicing in praise. *R*

Liturgy of the Hours, adapted

10b Evening

The Son of God is coming with great power : all mankind
shall see his face and be reborn.

R **Be near us, Lord, today.**

You will bring us wisdom, fresh understanding and
new vision. *R*

You will bring us good news, and power which will
transform our lives. *R*

You will bring us truth, showing us the way to
our Father. *R*

Born of a woman in our flesh, you will open the way to
eternal life and joy. *R*

Liturgy of the Hours, adapted

CHRISTMAS EVE

10c Morning and Evening

Today you will know that the Lord will come to deliver us :
in the morning you shall behold his glory.

R **Lord, turn our mourning into dancing.**

Today the iniquity of the earth will be blotted out : and in
the morning the Saviour will reign over us.   *R*

Today justice will look down from heaven : and in the
morning truth shall flourish out of the earth.   *R*

Today mercy and truth shall meet together : and in the
morning righteousness and peace will embrace.   *R*

Today the Lord will delight in you : and in the morning your
land shall have its wedding.   *R*

Tonight when peaceful silence lies over the world : we shall
wait for your mighty Word to leap down to earth from your
heavenly throne.   *R*

Compiler

CHRISTMAS DAY to day before Naming of Jesus

11a Morning

God our Father, this morning we eagerly greet the birth of Jesus, our brother and Saviour. He is our Daystar from on high, the light-bearer who brings the dawn to us who wait patiently for his coming.

R   **Glory to God in the highest, and peace in all the earth!**

Father, on this holy day bless the Church all over the world : may she light afresh in our hearts the lamps of hope and peace. **R**

Your Son has come to us in the fullness of time : let those who wait for him recognize his coming. **R**

His birth bound heaven to earth in harmony and peace : establish that same peace among the nations and between ourselves today. **R**

With Mary and Joseph we rejoice in the birth of Jesus : may we welcome Christ as they did. **R**

Liturgy of the Hours, adapted

11b Evening

Today the angels' message rings through the world. Gathered together in prayer, we rejoice in the birth of our brother, the Saviour of all.

R   **Lord Jesus, in your birth is our peace.**

May our lives express what we celebrate at Christmas : may its mystery enrich your Church this year.   **R**

We join the shepherds in adoring you : we kneel before you, holy child of Bethlehem.   **R**

We pray for the shepherds of your Church : be close to them as they proclaim your birth to mankind.   **R**

As we travel on our earthly pilgrimage, may your light shine in our hearts : and may we see you in glory, born in our midst.   **R**

Word of the Father, you became man for us, and raised us to a new life : may the dead share with us in the new birth which Christmas proclaims.   **R**

Liturgy of the Hours, adapted

NAMING OF JESUS to EPIPHANY

12a Morning

O Christ, splendour of the Father's glory, sustaining all the worlds by your Word of power : we pray that our lives may ever be renewed by your presence.

R **Son of the living God, have mercy upon us.**

O Christ, born into the world in the fullness of time for the salvation and liberation of every creature : we pray that all may come to their rightful freedom. **R**

O Christ, begotten of the Father before all time, born in the stable at Bethlehem : we pray that your Church may be a sign of poverty and joy. **R**

O Christ, true God and true man, born in a people to fulfil their expectations : may all find their desires fulfilled in you. **R**

O Christ, child of the Virgin Mary, wonderful in Counsel, mighty Lord, eternal God, Prince of Peace : we pray that the whole world may live in peace and justice. **R**

Taizé

12b Evening

Almighty God, you have never forsaken the world when it abandoned you : from ancient times you made the promise of your victory shine before your People:

R **The joy of our hearts is in God!**

The patriarchs hoped for your Christ : Abraham rejoiced to see his day, foretold by the prophets and desired by all the nations. **R**

The heavenly host celebrated his birth : apostles, martyrs and the faithful throughout the ages have repeated the angels' song, and now we with your whole Church praise you, for our eyes have seen your salvation. **R**

Son of God, you became poor to make many rich : you humbled yourself and took the form of a slave, lifting us up to share in your glory. **R**

We were in darkness and you have given us light and strength : we were without hope and we have received from your fullness grace upon grace. **R**

Dispose of us as you will; make us a People who serve you in holiness : give us honest hearts to hear your word and produce in us abundant fruit to your glory. **R**

Taizé

EPIPHANY to EPIPHANY 1

13a Morning

Today the Wise Men knelt before our Saviour. Let us also worship him with great joy.

R **Light of light, reveal yourself this day.**

Christ manifested in the flesh : sanctify us by the Word of God and by prayer.   *R*

Christ, vindicated in the Spirit : free our lives from the spirit of discord.   *R*

Christ, seen by angels : give us even now a share in the joy of heaven.   *R*

Christ, preached among the nations : move all hearts by the power of your Spirit.   *R*

Christ, believed in by the world : renew your disciples' faith.   *R*

Christ, taken up in glory : enkindle in us the desire of your kingdom.   *R*

Liturgy of the Hours, adapted

13b Evening

Lord Jesus, in your epiphany you were revealed to the world as the Son of God, the promised Saviour to the nations.

R   **Lord, show us the light of your face.**

You were revealed to all nations by the visit of the Wise Men, who offered you their treasures : make our lives an acceptable gift to you.   *R*

You were revealed in the first of your signs by turning water into wine : refresh us continually by your presence in our hearts.   *R*

You were revealed in becoming sin for us under the Law by being baptized in John : we give thanks that in baptism we are set free to live the life of the Spirit.   *R*

You were revealed at your baptism by the descent of the Spirit as a dove, and the voice of the Father : may we never fail to acknowledge that divine Sonship in our faith.   *R*

Were you revealed to us in all your glory, we could never endure it : when we pass from this earthly life may we be found worthy to gaze on that glory without fear.   *R*

Compiler

14a Morning

We give thanks to Christ, the Lord, who died on the cross
that we might live. Let us pray to him with all our heart.

R **Lord, Jesus, may your death bring us to life.**

Master and Saviour, you have taught us by your life and
renewed us by your passion : prevent us from growing used
to sin.   *R*

You call on us to feed the hungry : let us deny ourselves
some food this day to sustain our brothers and sisters in
their need.   *R*

May we accept from your hands this day of Lent : let us
make it yours by deeds of love.   *R*

End the rebellion within our hearts : make us generous and
willing to share.   *R*

Liturgy of the Hours

14b Evening

We call upon you, Lord God: you know everything, nothing escapes from you, Master of all truth.

R **Be my rock and my fortress, O Lord!**

You have made all the worlds and you watch over every creature : you guide to the way of life, all who are living in darkness and the shadow of death. *R*

It is your will to save everyone in the world, and to bring them to fullness : we offer you our praise and thanks, glorifying you with heart and voice. *R*

It was your will to call us, instructing us and opening the way for us to follow : you have given us wisdom and understanding for eternal life. *R*

You have ransomed us from the slavery of sin, in spite of all our wanderings, by the precious blood of your only Son : and you have given us glory and freedom. *R*

We were dead and you gave us new birth by the Spirit : we were sinners and you gave us pure hearts. *R*

Taizé

LENT 3 to day before Lent 5
SUNDAYS AND WEEKDAYS
15a Morning

Let us pray earnestly to Christ our Saviour, who redeemed us by his death and resurrection.

R **Lord, have mercy upon us.**

You went up to Jerusalem to endure the passion and enter into glory : lead your Church into the paschal feast of eternal life. *R*

Your heart was pierced with a lance : heal the wounds of our human weakness. *R*

You made your cross the tree of life : share your victory with all the baptized. *R*

You gave salvation to the repentant thief : pardon all our sins. *R*

Liturgy of the Hours, adapted

15b Evening

Let us call on the name of the Lord Jesus who saves his people from their sins.

R **Jesus, son of David, have mercy upon us.**

Christ our Lord, you gave yourself up for the Church to make her holy : renew her once more through the spirit of repentance. *R*

Good master, reveal to young people that way of life which you have planned for each one of them : may they be faithful to your call and obey your will for them. *R*

Give hope to the sick and restore them to health : help us to comfort and take care of them. *R*

In baptism you made us children of the Father : may we live for you now and always. *R*

Grant to the faithful departed peace and glory : let us reign with them one day in your heavenly kingdom. *R*

Liturgy of the Hours, adapted

LENT 5 to Wednesday in Holy Week
SUNDAYS AND WEEKDAYS

16a Morning

Let us implore our Redeemer, who suffered his passion, was buried and rose again from the dead, saying,

R **O Christ, we adore you.**

Lord our Master, for us you became obedient unto death : teach us to do your Father's will. *R*

Lord our Life, by dying on the cross you have conquered death and the powers of darkness : enable us to share in your death and resurrection into glory. *R*

Lord our Strength, you were despised by men, humiliated as a condemned criminal : teach us true humility. *R*

Lord our Salvation, you gave your life for love of your brothers : teach us to love one another with that same love. *R*

Lord our Lord, with hands outstretched on the cross, you draw all to yourself : gather into your kingdom all the scattered children of God. *R*

Taizé

16b Evening

Lord, you turned your face to Jerusalem to bear the cross and the shame : let us follow you as your disciples faithfully to the end.

R **Lead us, Lord, into the Holy City.**

On the way to Jerusalem you raised Lazarus from the dead : raise us from the death of sin to the life of righteousness. *R*

You promised that when you were lifted up from this earth you would draw everyone to yourself : reign for ever in every human heart. *R*

You rode on a colt and entered the Holy City in lowly triumph : give us the grace to tread the path of humility. *R*

The children of the Hebrews tore branches from the trees in your honour : may we ever hail you as our King with our whole hearts. *R*

The Father glorified your name as you drank the cup that he willed : give us the will to drink of that cup and endure his baptism. *R*

Compiler

MAUNDY THURSDAY

17a Morning

Let us think on Jesus, the Lord : instead of the joy meant for him, he endured the cross, ignoring its disgrace.

R **We worship you, Lord, upon the cross.**

You went about among us, doing good : proclaiming the good news to the poor and freedom to prisoners. *R*

You came to loose the chains of every slavery : friend of the humble, bread of hungry souls, healer of the sick. *R*

Jesus, pattern of patience and goodness, prophet of the Kingdom of God, Master, gentle and humble of heart : forgiving all who loved much and calling the weary and the burdened. *R*

Jesus, you came into the world to serve and to lay down your life : you had nowhere to lay your head, you were betrayed for money, dragged before Pilate and nailed to the cross. *R*

Jesus, Lord of all the worlds by your resurrection from the dead : alive for ever to intercede with your Father and ours. *R*

Taizé

17b Evening

Let us adore our Saviour, who at the Last Supper, on the night he was betrayed, entrusted to the Church the memorial of his death and resurrection to be celebrated throughout the ages. Confident that he will hear us, we pray,

R   **Sanctify the people whom you redeemed by your blood.**

Christ, our Redeemer, let us share in your passion by works of penance : let us attain the glory of your resurrection.   *R*

Grant us the protection of your Mother, the comforter of the afflicted : may we bring to others the consolation you have given us.   *R*

Unite the faithful to your passion in times of trouble and distress : let the power of your salvation shine forth in their lives.   *R*

You humbled yourself even to accepting death, death on a cross : grant to your servants obedience and patience.   *R*

Share with the dead your bodily glory : let us rejoice one day with them in the fellowship of the saints.   *R*

Liturgy of the Hours

GOOD FRIDAY • HOLY CROSS DAY

18a Morning

Let us enter the passion of our Lord as he treads the way of
sorrows; and glory in his cross as he wins the victory over
sin and death, as we pray,

All trials and questionings

R **Let us bear for you, Lord.**

All mocking and scoffing *R*

All taunts and scepticism *R*

All pain and weariness *R*

All loneliness and dereliction *R*

All betrayal and reviling *R*

All humiliation and defeat *R*

All violence and cruelty *R*

Compiler

18b Evening

Father, forgive them, for they know not what they do :
Father, forgive all who sin in blindness and ignorance.

R **Father, into your hands we commit our spirit.**

Truly I say to you, today you will be with me in Paradise :
Lord, through your Church, hold out to all humanity the
reward of everlasting life.   **R**

Woman, behold your son; behold your mother :
Lord, assure us of the protection and prayers of your Mother
and all the saints.   **R**

I thirst : Lord, satisfy all who hunger and thirst for
righteousness' sake.   **R**

My God, my God, why have you forsaken me? : Lord, make
your healing presence known to the desolate and all
in despair.   **R**

It is finished : Lord, accomplish the number of your elect and
hasten your Kingdom at the end of time.   **R**

Compiler

EASTER EVE

19a Morning

Let us implore our Redeemer who suffered his passion, was buried and rose again from the dead, saying,

R **O Christ, we adore you.**

O Saviour Christ, your grief-stricken Mother was present at your cross and burial : enable us to share in your passion at our times of testing. *R*

O Lord Christ, like the seed of wheat fallen into the ground, you have borne the fruit of the life of God : may we die to sin and live for God. *R*

O Christ the new Adam, you descended into the kingdom of the dead to set the good free from captivity : may your voice be heard by all who have died in sin that they may live. *R*

O Christ, Son of the living God, through baptism we have been buried with you in death : make us partners in your resurrection, that we may walk in the newness of life. *R*

Taizé

19b Evening

Let us implore our Redeemer who suffered his passion, was buried and rose again from the dead, saying,

R   **O Christ, we adore you.**

Lord Jesus, from your side pierced by the spear poured water and blood, in token of the birth of your Church : by your death, your burial and your resurrection, give life to your people.   **R**

Lord Jesus, you remembered those who had forgotten the promise of your resurrection : remember too those who live without hope, knowing nothing of the resurrection.   **R**

Lamb of God, our Passover, you were sacrificed for all : draw all people to yourself.   **R**

God of the universe, whom the whole world cannot contain, you were willing to be enclosed in the tomb : preserve all from eternal death and give us glorious immortality.   **R**

O Christ, Son of the living God, you descended into the dwelling of the dead; have pity on all who like yourself have known death and the grave : and let us all share the glory of your resurrection.   **R**

Taizé

EASTER DAY to ASCENSION
SUNDAYS AND WEEKDAYS (Alternative A)
BAPTISM • CONFIRMATION

20a Morning

Heavenly Father, in the waters of the Red Sea the Hebrews became your people : may the baptismal waters of Easter and the Light of Christ always renew our baptism into him.

R **Lord, make us an Easter people.**

As with the your power the Hebrews escaped from the tyranny of Pharaoh : so may we through the Paschal Mystery break with the tyranny of sin. *R*

As Christ died and lay buried in the depths of the tomb : may all the baptized bury their sin, and die for ever to the old Adam within. *R*

As Christ burst from the tomb on the third day and could not be constrained by the powers of death : so may we rejoice in the liberating power of Easter, set free to rise to new life. *R*

Let us pray for the newly baptized and all preparing to enter the Church's fellowship by baptism and confirmation : may they shine as a light in the world to your eternal glory. *R*

Compiler

20b Evening

Risen Lord, on the first day of the week the women came to anoint your body, but were sent to tell the disciples of your resurrection : as the resurrection people may we always be sharing this news.

R **Alleluia is our song!**

The disciples who journeyed to Emmaus did not at first recognize you : enable us to see you in the lives of others and at work in the world around us. *R*

Like Thomas we are often haunted by doubts : give us the joy and grace to live the risen life by faith and not by sight. *R*

At your command the disciples cast their nets and made a huge catch of fish : may we never forget that all things are possible with you. *R*

Beside the tomb Mary Magdalen tried to touch you : may all who suffer feel your healing touch tonight. *R*

The angels at the empty tomb told the women not to seek the living among the dead : raise all the departed on the last day to a glorious resurrection. *R*

Compiler

EASTER DAY to ASCENSION
SUNDAYS AND WEEKDAYS (Alternative B)
BAPTISM • CONFIRMATION

21a Morning

Let us pray with confidence to God our Father. In Christ he has given all his children the pledge of resurrection.

R   **Lord, grant us the blessing of your resurrection.**

Father, by a pillar of fire you led your people through the desert : may the risen Christ be the light of our lives.   *R*

Through the voice of Moses you spoke on the mountain : may the risen Christ be our word of life.   *R*

With the gift of manna you fed your wandering people : may the risen Christ be our bread from heaven.   *R*

You drew water from the rock to save your children : may the risen Christ fill us with his Spirit.   *R*

Liturgy of the Hours, adapted

21b Evening

Let us pray to Christ, who by his resurrection strengthens his people in hope.

R   **Ever living Christ, hear us.**

Lord Jesus, from your opened side there poured out blood and water : cleanse the Church, your bride, from every stain of sin.   *R*

Good shepherd, risen from the dead, you gave to the apostle Peter the care of your flock : may our bishops be ever strengthened in charity and zeal.   *R*

Beside the lake of Galilee you directed your disciples to a great catch of fish : direct the work of your disciples today, and give them your abundant blessing.   *R*

On the shore of the lake you prepared food for your disciples : help us to find your joy in caring for others.   *R*

Jesus, the Last Adam, life-giving Spirit, conform the dead to your likeness : make their joy complete.   *R*

Liturgy of the Hours, adapted

ASCENSION DAY • SUNDAY
AFTER ASCENSION
CHRIST THE KING (Morning 22c)

22a Morning

Let us pray to the Lord who is now lifted up from the earth, drawing all things to himself.

R **You, Christ, are the King of glory.**

Lord Jesus, you offered one sacrifice for sin and then ascended in victory to the Father : achieve the eternal perfection of those whom you are sanctifying.   *R*

Eternal priest, minister of the new covenant, you are alive and interceding for us : save your people who turn to you in prayer.   *R*

After your passion you appeared to your disciples and they knew you to be alive : inspire us to believe that you are with us today.   *R*

On this day you promised the Holy Spirit to your apostles, for the spreading of your gospel to the ends of the earth : strengthen us by the power of the Spirit in bearing witness before the world.   *R*

Liturgy of the Hours, adapted

22b Evening

Rejoicing, let us pray to Christ who is seated at the right hand of the Father.

R **The Lord is king, let earth rejoice!**

King of glory, in you our mortal flesh has been lifted to the heights : deliver us from the corruption of sin and restore us to immortal life. **R**

Following the path of love, you came down to us from heaven : let us follow that same path in our ascent to you. **R**

You promised to draw all people to yourself : graft us into your body like branches of the vine. **R**

You have ascended into heaven : let us be there with you in our minds and hearts. **R**

We await your coming in majesty on the great day of judgement : then may we gaze on you in glory with all the faithful departed. **R**

Liturgy of the Hours, adapted

CHRIST THE KING

22c Morning

Let us pray with joy to Christ at the right hand of the Father, saying

R **You are the King of Glory!**

You have raised the weakness of our flesh, heal us from our sins : restore us to the full dignity of our life. **R**

May our faith lead us to the Father : as we follow the road you trod. **R**

You have promised to draw all to yourself : let none of us stay separate from your Body. **R**

Grant that by our longing we may join you in your kingdom : where your humanity and ours is glorified. **R**

You are the true God, and you will be our judge : so lead us to contemplate your tender mercy. **R**

Taizé

DAY AFTER ASCENSION to day before
Pentecost
GUIDANCE OF THE HOLY SPIRIT

23a Morning

Our Lord Jesus Christ ascended into the heavens to prepare a place for us and to send us the Spirit who would lead us into all truth. Let us ask him for a renewal of the gifts of the Spirit:

For the Spirit of wisdom

R **Let us earnestly pray.**

For the Spirit of understanding   *R*

For the Spirit of counsel   *R*

For the Spirit of inward strength   *R*

For the Spirit of knowledge   *R*

For the Spirit of true godliness   *R*

For the Spirit of the fear of the Lord   *R*

Compiler

23b Evening

As we await the coming of the Holy Spirit let us ask the Lord to enrich us with the fruits of the Spirit :

Lord of love, send us the Spirit of love that endures and will never pass away.

R **Lord, you chose us to bear much fruit.**

Lord of joy, send us the Spirit of joy which no one can take from us. *R*

Lord of peace, send us the Spirit of peace that passes all understanding. *R*

Lord of patience, send us the Spirit of patience that bears all things. *R*

Lord of kindness, send us the Spirit of kindness that accepts friend and enemy alike. *R*

Lord of goodness, send us the Spirit of goodness that gives in full measure. *R*

Lord of faithfulness, send us the Spirit of faithfulness that remains steadfast unto death. *R*

Lord of gentleness, send us the Spirit of gentleness that turns away anger. *R*

Lord of self-control, send us the Spirit of self-control to overcome the snares of the devil. *R*

Compiler

PENTECOST • GUIDANCE OF THE HOLY SPIRIT • BAPTISM • CONFIRMATION

24a Morning

Holy Spirit, Creator! In the beginning, you moved over the waters and from your breath all creatures drew their life. Without you every living creature turns to dust.

R **Holy Spirit, come!**

Holy Spirit, Counsellor! By your inspiration the people of God and the prophets spoke and acted in faith. You clothed them in your power, to be bearers of your Word. *R*

Holy Spirit, Power! You overshadowed the Virgin Mary, to make her the mother of the Son of God. You prepared a pure dwelling to receive him. *R*

Holy Spirit, Sanctifier! By you, Jesus grew in wisdom and grace. On the day of his baptism, you descended on him as a dove to consecrate him, and you armed him with power to bear witness to the Father. *R*

Taizé

24b Evening

Living God! Come and make our bodies temples of your Holy Spirit. Baptize with fire your whole Church, that we may stand in the world as a pillar of your love.

R **Strengthen us, Holy Spirit!**

Give to us all the fruits of the Spirit : love for all, joy, peace, patience, kindness, faithfulness. *R*

May your Spirit speak through your servants who live by your Word of truth. *R*

Send the Comforter to all who are passing through adversity, or are victims of human wickedness. *R*

Preserve from hatred and war every nation, every people, and create a new brotherhood among us by the power of your communion. *R*

Holy Spirit, Lord and Source of Life, giver of many gifts. *R*

Spirit of wisdom and knowledge; Spirit of counsel and of might. *R*

Spirit of understanding and of prayer; Spirit of obedience. *R*

Taizé

TRINITY SUNDAY

25a Morning

Let us celebrate the wonder of the Holy and undivided
Trinity, three Persons and one God, the Trinity of eternal
and mutual love; with the cherubim and seraphim we pray,

R **Heaven and earth are full of your glory.**

Appearing as three angels, you promised Abraham and
Sarah in their old age the child, Isaac : lead us to a
knowledge of your great purpose in all things. ***R***

Throughout the ages the faith of the Church has been
confessed in Father, Son and Holy Spirit : we pray for the
grace to keep this faith intact and to treasure it. ***R***

Jesus, you commanded us to baptize all nations in the name
of Father, Son and Holy Spirit : may we know the joy of
sharing this faith with others. ***R***

O God, you are without beginning or end, and you give
everything its life and existence : in your infinite greatness,
look with mercy on our smallness. ***R***

Compiler

25b Evening

With the Church on earth and the Saints in heaven let us give endless praise to the Holy Trinity, to God the Creator, Redeemer and Sustainer of all: on whom we long to gaze in wonder.

R **Holy, Holy, Holy are you Lord, our God.**

Let us praise God the Father for the strength and goodness of fatherhood. *R*

Let us praise God the Son for the wisdom and kindness of motherhood. *R*

Let us praise the Holy Spirit for the light and grace of blessed love. *R*

Let us praise the Blessed Trinity for the uncreated, sovereign truth, wisdom and love. *R*

Let us praise the Blessed Trinity that humankind is his creation and his delight. *R*

Compiler (based on Julian of Norwich)

PRESENTATION OF CHRIST

26a Morning

Let us give thanks for God made man in Jesus Christ, on this day when the Lord enters his temple with great glory.

R **The light of Christ has come into the world.**

Lord, you are the chief cornerstone rejected by the builders : build us into that temple made without hands, a royal priesthood. *R*

Lord, you stand at the door of our hearts knocking : let us be open to receive your light, and shine as a light in the world. *R*

Lord, you were destined to become a sign of rejection and the rising and fall of many : give your comfort to all in distress. *R*

Mary and Joseph made the offering according to the Law when you were presented in the temple : may our lives be an offering according to the law of love. *R*

Compiler

26b Evening

Let us rejoice with Mary, the most blessed of all women, on this feast of her purification. We praise you Lord for the wonderful mystery of the Incarnation.

R **We rejoice to see your salvation.**

In Simeon the old covenant began to give place to the new in Jesus Christ : renew our faith each day within us. **R**

Simeon prophesied that a sword would pierce Mary's heart : grant that our faith may be purified by the trials of daily life. **R**

Simeon sang your praise when he saw the promised Lord : may our lives be a continual act of praise. **R**

We give thanks for the constancy and faith of Simeon and Anna : make us steadfast in the faith when we become discouraged and downhearted. **R**

Anna spread the word that the Saviour had come into the world : make us glad to spread the good news of your kingdom. **R**

Compiler

ST JOSEPH

27a **Morning**

Whatever we do or say, let us do it in the name of the Lord Jesus, giving thanks to God the Father through him.

R **Lord, hear us.**

As Joseph believed what you had told him and became the guardian of your only Son : so may we put our faith in you, and receive the fulfilment of your promise. *R*

Father, give us that faith which gives substance to our hopes : convince us of the truth we do not comprehend. *R*

Joseph took the child Jesus into his care, loving and accepting him as his own Son : may we accept all that God gives us, and care for those entrusted to us. *R*

You have given mankind authority over the work of your hands and invited him to share in your creation : help us to accept our responsibility by working for your glory and the good of all humanity. *R*

Liturgy of the Hours, adapted

27b Evening

Let us pray to God our Father, for from him all fatherhood in heaven and on earth takes its name.

R **Father, hallowed be your name.**

Father, in your Son you revealed to Joseph the mystery kept secret for endless ages : help us to acknowledge your Son as God and Man. **R**

Father, you enabled Joseph to spend his life in your service : set our minds on your kingdom and your justice before all other things. **R**

Father, your will is that everyone should accept and answer your call : by the example of Joseph, give us the grace to live in accord with your will. **R**

Creator of all things, you have entrusted your work to our hands : grant that our labours may prove worthy of you. **R**

Father, in whom all men and women live, grant to those who have died new life : through your Son, with Mary and Joseph, and all your saints for ever. **R**

Liturgy of the Hours, adapted

ANNUNCIATION • VISIT OF MARY TO ELIZABETH

28a Morning

The prophets foretold that a virgin should conceive and bear a son, the Lord Emmanuel : so the angel of the Lord appeared to Mary and she conceived by the Holy Spirit.

R   **Blessed are those who hear and keep your word, O God.**

Mary said, I am the Lord's servant : be it unto me according to your Word.   *R*

He is called the Wonderful Counsellor : the Mighty God, the Prince of Peace.   *R*

The Word was made flesh and lived among us : and we beheld his glory, the glory of the Father.   *R*

The Law came through Moses : grace and truth have now come through Jesus Christ.   *R*

Compiler

28b Evening

Lord, your unchanging plan is from everlasting, and from the beginning you willed your Son to be born a man on earth, of the Virgin Mary by the Spirit of the Most High.

R   **Incarnate Lord, come and live in our hearts.**

As the angel brought the glad tidings to Mary, so we rejoice with her that she shared her good news with Elizabeth : Lord, guard us from speaking any evil.   *R*

Daily with Mary we proclaim the greatness of the Lord : let us always give thanks for the great things he has done for his people.   *R*

The child in the womb leaped for joy when the news of the Saviour was brought : may all who have doubt and difficulty in believing come to know that joy.   *R*

How beautiful on the mountains are the feet of those who bring the Gospel of peace : as we pray for all who hear bad news at this time, may they know the consolation of your love.   *R*

Mary brought great joy to Elizabeth by her visitation : may we too, discover that joy in all our daily encounters with others.   *R*

Compiler

JOHN THE BAPTIST (both feasts)

29a Morning

John the Forerunner was wonderfully born to turn the hearts of the disobedient to the wisdom of the just : Lord, make straight your way in our hearts.

R **Let us behold the Lamb of God.**

John lived in the wilderness and was content with little : in a world of greed help us to live with greater simplicity.   *R*

John preached truth and justice, and was imprisoned and beheaded : make us bold to condemn injustice when we see it.   *R*

John warned that the axe was laid to the root and the time for repentance had come : give us a spirit of deepening penitence.   *R*

John was sent to point out the Lamb of God : make us fearless to point out to the world its loving Saviour.   *R*

Compiler

29b Evening

John the Baptist was given the task of preparing your way, Lord Jesus : may we, too, be prepared for your coming in glory.

R   **Lord, let us prepare your path.**

John, the greatest of the prophets, knew that he must decrease : increase your presence in our hearts and your power in our lives.   *R*

John was unworthy to unloose your shoe, yet you washed your disciples' feet : may we be willing to serve others in the humblest ways.   *R*

John baptized with water : may we who have been baptized into Christ be filled with the fire of the Holy Spirit.   *R*

John heard your voice and witnessed the descent of the Spirit : may we ever proclaim Christ as Lord.   *R*

John came in the spirit and power of Elijah : when we are weak, come into our hearts with all your strength.   *R*

Compiler

TRANSFIGURATION

30a Morning

Loving Father, you transfigured your loving Son and
revealed the Holy Spirit in the bright cloud : enable us to
hear the word of Christ with faithful hearts.

R **May we do everything for your glory.**

You made light to rise in the darkness, and you have shone
in our hearts, to make known your glory in the face of
Christ : revive in us the spirit of contemplation. *R*

You have called us by your grace, revealed in the appearing
of our Saviour Jesus Christ : make life and immortality blaze
among us by your Gospel. *R*

You have given us your great love, and we are called your
children : when Christ is revealed, may we be like him,
seeing him as he is. *R*

Taizé, adapted

30b Evening

O Christ, by your transfiguration you revealed the resurrection to your disciples before your passion began : we pray for the Church in all the difficulties of the world; in our trials may we be transfigured by the joy of your victory.

R **Lighten our darkness, O Lord.**

O Christ, you took your friends with you and led them to a high mountain : may your Church stay close to you, in the peace and hope of your glory. **R**

O Christ, you led Peter, James and John down from the mountain and into the suffering world : when our hearts crave permanence may we know the permanence of your love as you take us with you on your way. **R**

O Christ, you lightened the earth when the Creator's glory rose upon you : we pray to you for all; may the nations come to the light. **R**

O Christ, you will transfigure our poor bodies and conform them to your glorious body : we pray to you for our brothers and sisters, that they may be changed into your likeness, from glory to glory. **R**

Taizé, adapted

BLESSED VIRGIN MARY (Conception, Nativity, Falling Asleep)

31a Morning

Father, you chose Mary from the beginning to be the mother of your incarnate Word : grant that we may bear that same Word to all whom we meet today.

R   **With all generations we call her blessed.**

Father, we rejoice in the birth of the Blessed Virgin, the dawn of our salvation : lead us into the glorious day of rebirth held out to us by her Son.   *R*

Elizabeth was honoured by a visit from the mother of her Lord : may we find equal joy in the presence of our Lady and all the saints in the life of the Church.   *R*

When the child Jesus was lost in the temple, Mary and Joseph found him : rescue all who are confused and have lost their way in life.   *R*

At the wedding at Cana Mary said, 'They have no wine' : of your goodness fill all who suffer starvation and deprivation with your abundant life.   *R*

Compiler

31b Evening

Lord, after your ascension the disciples returned to
Jerusalem, and Mary continued to live and pray with them in
the life of the Church : may all Christians acknowledge her
special place in the Church, and give her due honour.

R   **Hail Mary, blessed are you among women.**

Lord, Mary was obedient to the Father's command to become
your mother : make all Christian people obedient to your
will and true to their vocation.   *R*

At your conception, Mary remained a virgin and lived a life
of simplicity : give to all who are rich, poverty of spirit, and
to all who are destitute, the fulfilment of their needs.   *R*

On the cross you gave Mary into the protection of John, the
beloved disciple : protect the weak, the vulnerable and all in
any kind of danger tonight.   *R*

A woman appeared crowned with the stars and the moon at
her feet : remember the promise to your people that they
should reign with you forever.   *R*

Your mother has taken her place beside you in heaven : fulfil
your promise to the departed that we shall rise again in a
glorious body.   *R*

Compiler

MICHAELMAS

32a Morning

Lord of all creation, an angel foretold your birth and the birth of many of your chosen servants : let us rejoice in the wonderful orders of angels.

R   **Holy, holy, holy is the Lord our God.**

Angels announced your birth to the shepherds with great joy and praise : may our lips be always praising you.   *R*

Angels ministered to you in your temptation and trial : be present, we pray, to all who are in trouble or oppression.   *R*

Angels announced your resurrection to Mary Magdalen : fill us with the assurance of your risen power.   *R*

Angels were present at your ascension into heaven : make us ready for your coming again in great glory.   *R*

Compiler

32b Evening

We praise you, O God, for the angels and archangels, cherubim and seraphim, thrones and dominations, virtues, powers and principalities.

R **Heaven and earth are full of your glory.**

With all the angels let us praise God for the archangel Gabriel, the messenger : make us attentive to the promptings of your Spirit. *R*

With all the angels let us praise God for the archangel Michael, vanquisher of Satan : with his aid may we tread down Satan under our feet. *R*

With all the angels let us praise God for the archangel Raphael, the angel of healing, as we remember before you all the sick. *R*

With all the angels let us praise God for the guardian angels, as we pray now for their protection in every danger. *R*

With all the angels let us offer our worship in the Spirit to the Father through the Son, and join our praises with the whole company of heaven. *R*

Compiler

ALL SAINTS • ANY SAINT

(Alternatives for Women saints see 39a and 39b)

33a Morning

Seeing we are surrounded by so great a cloud of witnesses, let us cast off everything that hinders us and run steadily the race that is set before us.

R   **Lord, lead us with the saints to glory everlasting.**

Lord, you filled the apostles with the Spirit to preach the gospel to every nation : enable us with the same Spirit to continue that work of proclamation.   *R*

The prophets brought hope to the people through your promises : grant that we may see those promises fulfilled in the world today.   *R*

The Church was founded on the blood of the martyrs : make us ever willing to die for the martyr's crown.   *R*

Lord, you sought the solitude of the mountains of Galilee : with all who have lived the solitary life let us find you in the silence of our hearts.   *R*

You committed your Church into the care of your shepherds, the bishops, throughout the ages : may all who seek refuge and solace find it in the Church.   *R*

Compiler

33b   Evening

With all faithful Christians we believe and trust in the communion of saints. Let us pray now to the Father amid that great fellowship and treasure their example.

For all the saints,

R   **We praise and magnify you, Lord.**

For all the saints who have served you in the monastic life,   *R*

For all the saints who have been notable for their works of charity and courage,   *R*

For all the saints who have set aside everything to love you above all things in the contemplative life,   *R*

For all the saints who as preachers and teachers have borne the light of your truth in all parts of the world,   *R*

For all the saints who have been faithful dispensers of Word and Sacrament,   *R*

Compiler

ALL SOULS • REMEMBRANCE • FUNERALS

34a Morning or Evening

Go forth from this world, Christian soul, in the name of
God, the omnipotent Father who created you.

R **Go forth on your journey, Christian soul.**

Go in the name of Jesus Christ, our Lord, Son of the living
God, who bled for you. *R*

Go in the name of the Holy Spirit, who has been poured out
for you. *R*

Go in the name of angels and archangels, thrones and
dominions, in the name of princedoms and powers, cherubim
and seraphim. *R*

Go in the name of patriarchs and prophets, apostles and
evangelists, in the name of martyrs and confessors, holy
virgins and all the saints of God. *R*

Go today to your place and be found there in peace, and
may your dwelling be in the Holy Mount of Zion. *R*

Traditional, adapted Compiler

34b Morning or Evening

Let us give thanks for the lives of all the departed in Christ (especially Nn) and praise God for their service to him and to others in their lives (and in their deaths).

R* **May all rise up rejoicing on the last day.**

Let us pray that the work of our redemption, begun and continued here on earth, may be completed in heaven. *R*

Let us pray that all the departed may be recreated in the image of the Creator, according to his will. *R*

Let us join with Christ in his everlasting intercession in heaven for all his children, living and departed. *R*

Let us pray that those of other faiths, and none, may finally be granted the vision of eternal glory in heaven. *R*

Let us pray for all who bear the grief of parting, either freshly or over many years, that they may know the healing of Christ's tender love. *R*

Compiler

*Alternative:

R   **Rest eternal grant unto them, O Lord, and let light perpetual shine upon them.**

CONVERSION OF ST PAUL
APOSTLES • EVANGELISTS

35a Morning and Evening

Lord, you were sent to the lost sheep of the house of Israel
and your apostles were sent to all the nations of the world:
may your Word dwell richly in us as we spread the Gospel;
and now we pray,

R **Send us out in the power of your Spirit.**

Lord, you said to Peter, Feed my sheep, tend my lambs : help
us to love you in those to whom we are sent. *R*

Lord, as the Good Shepherd, you lovingly sought the lost
sheep : give us a share of your joy when the lost are restored
to your fold. *R*

Lord, the master of the house spread a great banquet to
which many came : send us out to gather the poor and
unloved into the banquet in your kingdom. *R*

Lord, at Pentecost you filled the apostles with the Holy
Spirit : enable us to respond to that same Spirit as we enter
your service today. *R*

Lord, we honour the apostles as the witnesses to the
resurrection, who later bore witness in their own bodies :
give us the courage to witness boldly to our faith. *R*

Compiler

MISSIONARIES • MISSIONARY WORK
OF THE CHURCH

35b Morning and Evening

Lord, you commanded your apostles to make all nations
your disciples and to baptize them in the name of the Father,
Son and Holy Spirit : let us pray for all missionaries,
evangelists and preachers.

R **Make us faithful stewards of your word.**

Lord, the harvest is ready but the labourers are few : let us
bid the Lord of the harvest to send labourers to win a harvest
of souls. *R*

Lord, when the sower sowed his seed much was lost : give us
faith to believe that a rich harvest will finally
be gathered. *R*

The wheat grew secretly night and day until the full corn
appeared : give us patience and perseverance as we spread
your holy Word throughout the world. *R*

Lord, you sent your disciples to proclaim the kingdom,
healing the sick and giving sight to the blind : fill all who
suffer with your healing light and grace. *R*

Lord, it lay in your power to raise Lazarus from the dead :
fulfil your promise that all who die in you shall rise again at
the last day. *R*

Compiler

MARTYRS

36a Morning

Through the martyrs who were slain for God's word, let us give glory to our Saviour, the faithful and true Witness.

R **You redeemed us by your precious blood.**

Through the martyrs who bore witness to your love, set us free to live for you.   *R*

Through the martyrs who proclaimed your saving death, give us a deep and constant faith.   *R*

Through the martyrs who took up your cross, grant us courage for every trial.   *R*

Through the martyrs, washed in the blood of the Lamb, give us grace to conquer our weakness.   *R*

Liturgy of the Hours, adapted

36b Evening

Let us give thanks to the King of martyrs, for this is the hour when he offered himself in the Last Supper and laid down his life on the cross.

R   **We praise you, Christ the Lord.**

We praise you, Christ, our Saviour, example and strength of the martyrs : because you have loved us to the end,   *R*

Because you promised repentant sinners the reward of eternal life,   *R*

Because you have called the Church to offer the blood of the new and eternal covenant, the blood shed for the remission of sins,   *R*

Because you have brought us to this day with the gift of faith intact,   *R*

Because of the many brothers and sisters who today have come to share in your saving death,   *R*

Liturgy of the Hours, adapted

TIMOTHY AND TITUS • TEACHERS
BISHOPS • ABBOTS AND ABBESSES

37a Morning

Christ, the Good Shepherd, laid down his life for his sheep.
Let us praise him with grateful hearts, as we pray

R **Lord, nourish the lives of your people.**

Christ our Lord, in the holy pastors you reveal your love for
us : may we care for others with the care you show
through them.   **R**

Through your sacred ministers you are present in our midst
as the shepherd of our souls : constantly guide us by their
teaching and encouragement.   **R**

In the saints who lead your people, you manifest your power
of healing souls and bodies : remain with us always to renew
our lives in holiness.   **R**

By the example of the saints you instruct your faithful in the
ways of wisdom and love : through our pastors help us to
grow to the full stature of perfection.   **R**

Liturgy of the Hours, adapted

37b Evening

Let us pray to Christ, the High Priest, who was appointed to represent us to the Father.

R **Lord, save your people.**

Lord Jesus, in times past you have lighted the way for your people through wise and holy leaders : may Christians always enjoy this sign of your loving-kindness. *R*

You forgave the sins of your people when holy pastors prayed : continually cleanse your Church through their powerful intercession. *R*

In the presence of your brothers you anointed your holy ones and poured on them your Spirit : fill all the leaders of your Church with that same Spirit. *R*

Nothing could ever separate the holy pastors from your love : keep in safety those you redeemed by your passion. *R*

Through the pastors of your Church you give your sheep eternal life, and no one can steal them from you : save the faithful departed, for whom you laid down your life. *R*

Liturgy of the Hours, adapted

MYSTICS

38a Morning

Lord, you were led into the desert by the Spirit to be tempted by Satan : may your Spirit sustain us in the prayer of solitude.

R **Lord, set our hearts on fire with your love.**

In the desert you gave the Israelites water from the rock : refresh with your sweetness all who experience dryness in prayer. **R**

In the desert you provided meat and manna when your people were hungry : bless all involved in the work of spiritual guidance. **R**

You alone can make the desert bloom and draw honey from the rock : bless all who are beginning to seek you in the life of prayer. **R**

As we begin the day : give all Christian people an opportunity to pray as they work. **R**

Compiler

38b Evening

Lord, you withdrew to a lonely place with your disciples to pray : kindle in us a desire for stillness and silence where we may find you.

R **May we pray without ceasing.**

After feeding the multitude you sent the people away and remained alone : look with love on all who lead the solitary life. *R*

You asked the rich young man to give up everything and follow you : help us to make more room for you in our hearts. *R*

Lord, you commended Mary for choosing the better part : confirm in their calling all who devote their lives to contemplation. *R*

In your earthly ministry you healed many by faith and prayer : hear our prayer for all who suffer tonight. *R*

On the mountain you gave the disciples a burning vision of your glory : grant to all the departed to gaze on your glory for ever. *R*

Compiler

MARY MAGDALEN • WOMEN SAINTS

39a Morning

With all the holy women let us praise our Saviour and call on him in prayer.

R   **Come, Lord Jesus.**

Lord Jesus, you said of the woman who was a sinner, 'Her many sins are forgiven, because she has loved much' : grant us your forgiveness for our many sins.   *R*

Lord Jesus, women ministered to your needs on your saving journeys : open our eyes to see you in those who need our help.   *R*

Lord and master, Mary listened to your teaching, and Martha did the serving : may our faith grow ever deeper and our love go out to others.   *R*

Lord Jesus, you called those who do God's will, your brother and sister and mother : teach us to live as members of your family.   *R*

Liturgy of the Hours, adapted

40b Evening

Lord, you underwent a severe time of testing in the wilderness : let us pray for all trying their vocation to the sacred ministry.

R **Lord, send labourers into the harvest.**

Your call to the disciples was clear and penetrating : let us pray for all in authority who select the ministers of the Church.   *R*

The disciples often found your words hard and perplexing : let us pray for all in training for the ministry.   *R*

You spent much time teaching your disciples; to them you showed wisdom and patience : let us pray for all who train the ministers of the Church.   *R*

Lord, many came to hear you; some followed you and others could not accept your call : let us pray for the fostering of vocations to the ministry.   *R*

You commanded your disciples to bring peace to the places where they preached : let us pray for the newly ordained (commissioned) and the communities in which they serve.   *R*

Compiler

HARVEST THANKSGIVING

41a **Morning**

The heavens are telling the glory of God, and the earth rejoices in all his works; he has hollowed the depth of oceans and made them swarm with life : we praise you Lord for the harvest of the sea.

R **For your mercy is everlasting.**

He brings forth grass for flocks and herds and plants that are good to eat : we praise you Lord for the fruits of the earth. *R*

He has created the forest and shaped the plain for every kind of bird and beast : we praise you Lord for all earth's creatures. *R*

He has made the streams to spring from the mountains and hidden great riches in the rocks : we praise you Lord for mineral wealth. *R*

He gives us our tasks each morning and we work till evening comes : we praise you Lord for all who labour to win the harvest. *R*

Compiler

41b **Evening**

O Lord, how manifold are your works! In your wisdom you have created them all : the earth overflows with your marvellous gifts.

R **Lord, renew the face of the earth.**

All creatures look to you and you give them their food in due season : protect us from flood and drought. *R*

You visit the earth and lay your blessing upon it : make it abundant where harvest has failed. *R*

You crown the year with your bounty : may the wealth of earth and sea follow in your path. *R*

You soften the valleys with rain and give the land its fertility : we offer you our thanks and praise. *R*

You open your hand and our needs are amply supplied : make us ever attentive to those who cry to us in want. *R*

Compiler

CHRISTIAN UNITY

42a Morning

Lord, you prayed on earth that all your people should be one : hear us now as we pray for your divided Church.

R **May we all be one.**

Lead us through your Spirit into all truth. **R**

Lead us from ignorance and blindness to sight and true knowledge. **R**

Lead us to accept our fellow Christians in ever increasing charity. **R**

Unite all Christian people in your service now as we begin the work and witness of the day. **R**

Compiler

42b Evening

Lord, pride and arrogance have rent your Church asunder : forgive us our failures to follow the example of your love.

R **Where true love is found, you are dwelling there.**

Make us tolerant of what seems new and strange : open us, in the Spirit, to new directions. **R**

As we hold fast to a faith that is dear to us, enable it also to be broken, shared and more fully remade. **R**

Open our hearts and minds to the riches of other Christian traditions, that we may enrich our own. **R**

Make us feel the suffering of our divisions more keenly, that we may long to heal them more deeply. **R**

As we are all made one in death, unite us in the perfection of the resurrected life. **R**

Compiler

THANKSGIVING FOR HOLY COMMUNION

43a Morning

Lord of life, you are the true bread from heaven that comes down from God and gives life to the world : the bread you give is your own flesh.

R **You are the bread of life.**

Whoever comes to you, the bread of life, will never be hungry : whoever believes in you, will never be thirsty. *R*

Our ancestors ate manna in the desert and died : but whoever eats this bread will never die, but live for ever. *R*

Your flesh and blood are food and drink, indeed : whoever eats and drinks your body and blood dwells continually in you, and you in them. *R*

Whoever eats your flesh and drinks your blood possesses eternal life and will be raised up on the last day. *R*

Compiler

43b Evening

Lord Jesus, present to us in the eucharist, you saved your
people with manna from above when they journeyed in the
wilderness : yet now you save us with the bread of
everlasting life.

R   **Lord, give us this bread always.**

Lord, you fed them with the finest wheat and filled them
with honey from the rock : help us to love you more deeply
in the sacrament of the eucharist.   *R*

Beside the lake you satisfied a multitude with a few loaves
and still there remained plenty over : gladden us to give
thanks for the great riches of the sacramental life.   *R*

Lord, in the eucharist we offer you ordinary elements of
everyday life : but at your hands we receive them again as
priceless gifts, transformed by your glorious power.   *R*

Lord, you broke the bread at the Last Supper and shared it
among your disciples : may we also discover that sacred
unity that comes from sharing your body and blood.   *R*

The prophet gave the the starving widow the promise of life
when she shared her last loaf with him : we rejoice to taste
now of the heavenly banquet promised in the eucharist.   *R*

Compiler

SOCIAL RESPONSIBILITY

44a Morning

Gracious Father, you created the world with abundant riches, yet we have spoiled it with waste and filled it with want.

R **Lord have mercy.**

On the exploiter and the unscrupulous, *R*

On the greedy and the powerful, *R*

On the unjust and the oppressor, *R*

On every enemy of the truth, *R*

Compiler

44b Evening

Almighty Father, you put down the mighty and exalt the lowly : your prophets preached justice for the poor. Let us pray,

R   Your will be done, your kingdom come.

Give homes to the refugee and the poorly housed.   **R**

Fill the hungry with good things, and give them the means to provide for themselves.   **R**

Grant release to captives and prisoners of conscience.   **R**

To the whole human race bring the peace which passes all understanding.   **R**

In death we are empty and powerless : fill us with life in abundance in your heavenly kingdom.   **R**

Compiler

DEDICATION FESTIVAL • CHRISTIAN UNITY

45a Morning

Since we are living stones in the temple of Christ's body, let us pray to the Father for his beloved Church and profess our faith in her.

R* **This is the house of God, and the gate of heaven.**

Father, cleanse the vineyard of your Church : watch over it with care, and cultivate it with love until it fills the world and is wonderful to see.   *R*

Eternal shepherd, protect and extend the sheepfold of your Church : let there be one flock, with your Son its only shepherd.   *R*

Almighty Father, sow your Word in the field of the Church : produce its crop a hundredfold for your eternal harvest.   *R*

God of all wisdom, sanctify your house and all the members of your family : let mankind see the heavenly city, the new Jerusalem, the bride adorned with glory.   *R*

Liturgy of the Hours, adapted

*Alternative responses for CHRISTIAN UNITY:
R **Father, make us one in Christ.**
R **Holy Spirit, lead us into all truth.**

45b Evening

Let us pray to our Saviour who gave up his life to gather into unity the scattered children of God.

R* **Lord, remember your Church.**

Lord Jesus, you commanded your disciples to hear your words and put them into action : constantly strengthen your Church in faith, courage and trust.   *R*

Lord Jesus, there poured from your opened side blood and water : enliven your Church through the sacraments of the new and everlasting covenant.   *R*

Lord Jesus, you are present among those who are gathered in your name : hear your Church united in prayer.   *R*

Lord Jesus, you come with the Father to dwell in those who love you : perfect your Church all over the world in your divine love.   *R*

Lord Jesus, anyone who comes to you is never turned away : admit all those who have died into your Father's house.   *R*

Liturgy of the Hours, adapted

Appendices

Appendix 1 Chants for Canticles

Psalms for the Eucharist, ed. Stephen Foster, Vols 1–3. McCrimmon
Publishing Co. Ltd, 10–12 High Street, Great Wakering, Southend-on-Sea
SS3 0EQ. This provides a range of double chants intended for the Gradual
Psalms at the Eucharist, but just as easily used for canticles.
More chants for the Gradual Psalms; single and double chants, based on the
traditional Eight Tones, available from Society of St Francis, Brother Reginald,
15 Botolph Lane, Cambridge CB2 3RD.
Christus Rex, by Alan Wilson, Vol. 2 *The Song of Christ's Glory*, Vol. 3 *Bless
the Lord Great and Wonderful*, Vol. 4 *Glory and Honour*, Vol. 5 *Te Deum,
Saviour of the World*, Vol. 6 *Venite, Song of Creation*. Josef Weinberger Ltd;
obtainable from William Elkin Music Services, Station Road Industrial Estate,
Salhouse, Norwich NR13 6NY.

Appendix 2 Seasonal variations for the Invitatory Psalm

ADVENT Ps 24
CHRISTMAS to EPIPHANY Ps 100 as per ASB
EPIPHANY to LENT Ps 67
LENT Ps 95 *full* version as found in Psalter
EASTER to PENTECOST Easter Anthems as per ASB
SUNDAYS AFTER PENTECOST and MAJOR FESTIVALS Ps 100, *Jubilate*, as per
ASB
ALL OTHER OCCASIONS Ps 95 as per ASB

Appendix 3 Supplementary Psalms for the Seasons

ADVENT, Psalms of Ascent: 120–134
LENT, Penitential Psalms: 6, 32, 38, 51, 102, 130, 143
EASTER, *Hallel* Psalms: 113–118
SUNDAY MORNING, *Laudate* Psalms: 148, 150

Appendix 4 Suggestions for a Patristic Lectionary

From the Fathers to the Churches, ed. Brother Kenneth CGA. Collins.
Conformed to the ASB Calendar.
*The Cloud of Witnesses: A Companion to the Lesser Festivals and Holydays of
the ASB 1980*, ed. Michael Draper, with collects written by G.B. Timms.
Collins/Alcuin. See under 'Additional Reading' in that book.
The Joy of the Saints: Spiritual Readings throughout the Year, ed. Robert
Llewelyn. Darton, Longman & Todd.
Seasons of the Spirit, ed. Richard Harries. SPCK/Triangle.

Appendix 5 Table of Biblical References of Canticles

Also showing locations of other translations and other arrangements.
* indicates a reference to part of a canticle.
Any reference having no other location indicated is unique to this book, the work of the compiler.

		Canticle				
Ex 15.1–3,6,8–11,13	Canticle	25	LH	LHWE	DOR	CBAS
Deut 32.1–10a,13b,14		26	LH	LHWE	DOR	
I Sam 2.1–10		4	LH		DOR	
I Chron 29.10–13		2	LH		DOR	
Prov 9.1–6,10–12		37	LH			
Song of Songs 8.6–7		31				
Isa 2.2–5		8	LH		DOR	CBAS
Isa 9.2–7		11		SSF		
Isa 12.2–6		9	LH	SSF/ LHWE	DOR	CBAS
Isa 26.1–4,7–9,12		36	LH		DOR	
Isa 33.13–16		30	LH			
Isa 38.10–14,17–20		6	LH			
Isa 40.10–17		28	LH		DOR	CBAS
Isa 42.10–16a		3	LH		DOR	
Isa 49.8–13		39	LH			
Isa 52.7–10,1a		29				
Isa 53.2–6		21				CBAS
Isa 55.6–11		5		SSF	IPAF	CBAS
Isa 60.1–3,11,14,18,19		13		SSF		CBAS
Isa 61.6–9		43	LH			
Isa 61.10,11*		32	LH	SSF		
Isa 62.1–5*		32	LH	SSF		
Isa 63.1–3a,7,9		34		SSF		
Isa 66.10–14a		33	LH		DOR	
Jer 7.2–7		45	LH			
Jer 14.17–21		19	LH			
Jer 31.10–14		10	LH			CBAS
Lament 1.1–4		22				
Lament 3.19–30		23				
Lament 5.1–5,7–10,15		24				
Ezek 36.24–28		27	LH		DOR	CBAS
Ezek 47.1b*		66	RM			
Hosea 6.1–6		17		SSF	IPAF	
Joel 2.28*		68			DOR	
Hab 3.2–4,13a,15,16a,17–19		20	LH			
Tob 13.7–11,13–15		14	LH			
Judith 16.2–3,13–16		41	LH	SSF		
Wisd 3.1–8		35	LH			CBAS
Wisd 10.15–21		38				CBAS
Ecclus 36.11–17		44	LH			
Ecclus 39.13,22,14–16a		40	LH			
Song of the Three 3–7,11–18		15	LH			
Song of the Three 29–34		7	LH	SSF		CBAS
Song of the Three 35–68		18	LH	BCP		CBAS

	Canticle				
Prayer of Manasseh					
1a,2,4,6,7,9b–14	16		LHWE		
John 14.16,26*	68			DOR	
Rom 5.1–3,5,6,8*	65	IPAF		DOR	
Rom 8.26,28,29a,30,31b,32–35, 36b,37	60	IPAF			
	65				
	68			DOR	
I Cor 13.4–10,12,13*	50		SSF	DOR	
Eph 1.3–10	47	LH	SSF	DOR	CBAS
Phil 2.5–11	52	LH	SSF	DOR	CBAS
Col 1.12–20	49	LH	IPAF	DOR	CBAS
I Tim 3.16*	58	LH		DOR	
I Tim 6.15,16*	58				
I Pet 1.3,4,18–21	46		SSF		
I Pet 2.21–25	62	IPAF	SSF	DOR	
I John 4.7–8*	50		SSF	DOR	
I John 1.5–9	59		IPAF		
Rev 4.11*	48	LH	SSF		CBAS
Rev 5.9,10*	48	LH	SSF		CBAS
Rev 5.13	48				
	51				
	53				
Rev 7.9–10,14b–17	70		SSF		
Rev 11.17,18*	72	LH	SSF		
Rev 12.10–12a*	72	LH	SSF		
Rev 15.3,4	51	LH	SSF		
Rev 19.1b,2,5,6b,7,9*	53	LH	SSF	DOR	CBAS
Rev 21.1–5	71		SSF		
Rev 21.6b*	66	RM			
Rev 22.1,2*	66	RM			
Rev 22.12–14,16b,17,20	54		SSF		

Abbreviations:

BCP *Book of Common Prayer*
CBAS *Canadian Book of Alternative Services*
DOR *Daily Office Revised* (Joint Liturgical Group)
LH *Liturgy of the Hours* (Roman Breviary)
LHWE *Lent Holy Week and Easter*
IPAF *In Penitence and Faith*
RM *Roman Missal*
SSF *Franciscan Office Book*

Acknowledgements

The compiler wishes to express his thanks to the following for permission to reproduce or adapt material of which they are authors, publishers, or copyright holders.

Central Board of Finance of the Church of England for extracts from *The Alternative Service Book 1980* and *Lent, Holy Week and Easter, Prayers and Services*.

Geoffrey Chapman, an imprint of Cassell Publishers Ltd, for the *Ubi Caritas* by James Quinn SJ.

Mowbray for extracts from the Taizé Office, *Praise in All our Days*.

Oxford University Press for *A Song of the Incarnation*, paraphrased by Alan Luff from the New English Bible (NEB © 1970, Oxford and Cambridge University Presses).

Brother Reginald SSF, for his version of the Advent Prose, and for musical advice.

Revised English Bible © 1989, by permission of Oxford and Cambridge University Presses, and assistance from R.C. Coleman, Coordinating Editor.

The Ven. David Silk for extracts from *In Penitence and Faith* and *Prayers for Alternative Services*, and for a great deal of time and encouragement and inspiration, as well as the task of overseeing this book's compatibility with the ASB.

Sheila Upjohn for her canticle based on Julian of Norwich, commissioned for this book.

The Revd Michael Vasey for his canticle based on Anselm, from *In Penitence and Faith*.

A.P. Watt and Co. for extracts from *The Liturgy of the Hours* and the *Roman Missal*.

Also members of the Parmentergate Team Ministry for 'road-testing' much of the material comprising this book, Sheila Upjohn for proof-reading, and the Julian Shrine for photocopying facilities.

If the compiler has unwittingly transgressed any copyright, he makes sincere apologies and will acknowledge any such oversights in future editions.